Understanding Personality
and Motives of Women Managers

Research for Business Decisions, No. 16

Gunter Dufey, Series Editor
Professor of International Business and Finance
The University of Michigan

Other Titles in This Series

Understanding Personality
and Motives of Women Managers

by
Harish C. Tewari

RESEARCH PRESS

Produced and distributed by
UMI Research Press
an imprint of
University Microfilms International
Ann Arbor, Michigan 48106

Library of Congress Cataloging in Publication Data

Tewari, Harish C   1944-
    Understanding personality and motives of
women managers.

    (Research for business decisions ; no. 16)
    Originally presented as the author's thesis, University
of Cincinnati, 1977.
    Bibliography: p.
    Includes index.
    1. Women executives—Psychology. 2. Motivation
(Psychology)   I. Title. II. Series.

HF5500.2.T48 1979   158.7   79-22121
ISBN 0-8357-1055-6

IN MEMORY OF MY FATHER
Keshab Dutt Tewari

TABLE OF CONTENTS

TABLE OF CONTENTS

LIST OF TABLES

LIST OF TABLES

x

LIST OF TABLES

ACKNOWLEDGMENTS

Many people have given their assistance in completing this study. The author is indeed grateful for the patient guidance, understanding and the cooperation offered by his Chairman, Dr. Samuel J. Mantel, Jr., whose tremendous personal interest and influence will always remain a part of this thesis. The writer also wishes to express his sincere appreciation to Dr. Beverlee Anderson whose assistance and encouragement was extremely valuable. The other members of the committee, Dr. Caroline Boyer, Dr. John McKinney, and Dr. Evangeline Norton contributed the knowledge and research background enabling me to complete this study. Appreciation is also extended to Dr. Charles H. Scheidler for his timely suggestions. Ms. Elaine Torres deserves special thanks for her cooperation in typing this thesis. The writer is particularly grateful to all the companies and the sixty-one managers who agreed to participate in this study. It was through their generous cooperation that the study was made possible. Finally, the author is deeply indebted to his wife Veena for her patience, moral support, and inspiration during the course of the study.

CHAPTER I

INTRODUCTION

If Alexis de Tocqueville were visiting the United States today, he would be likely to describe our corporate order as "maleocracy", and no one would argue with the accuracy of his observation. A twentieth century de Tocqueville would also go on to note, with little fear of contradiction, that the attitudes on which this "maleocracy" is based are changing especially among a high proportion of the most influential men and women in this country. The walls of the corporate maleocracy are pretty thick and the weapons of those assaulting those walls are still not very powerful, in spite of growing dedication to tearing the walls down.[1]

Participation of Women in the Labor Force

Women workers constitute a little more than a third of the world's labor force. There are close to 40 million American women working, constituting 40 percent of the U.S. labor force.[2] The participation rates for young women have advanced considerably in recent years. By 1974 the rate had increased to 40 percent for ages 16 and 17, to 58 percent for those 18 and 19, and to 63 percent for those 20 to 24. Various social and economic factors have caused this rate to rise. An increasing proportion of young adult women have remained single. They have taken jobs after marriage, have postponed childbirth or "joined the labor force before their children started school." The expanding economy, and the equal employment legislation have provided various job opportunities to the young woman.[3] "The proportion of women, age 25 to 54, working or seeking work advanced from 37 percent in 1950 to 54 percent in 1974."[4] According to McEaddy:

> From 1950 to 1974, women 55 to 64 years of age accounted for only one third of the growth in the labor force, but they were four fifths of the women's labor force growth. However, the labor force participation rate for all older women, which had been increasing steadily between 1950 and 1970 has declined in the first half of the 1970's. From 1950 to 1970 the rate climbed from 19 to 25 percent; by 1974, it had declined to 23 percent largely due to the reduced participation of women 65 and over.[5]

Garfinkle reports that:

> during the 13 year period from 1962 to 1974, the long run tendency for the number of women in the labor force to increase faster than the number of men has continued. The passage of equal employment legislation in the mid-1960's and the increased recognition of women's capabilities has helped them to increase their proportionate share in a

number of occupations in which few have worked in the past. In the
broad category of professional occupations, women constitute 40
percent of all employees in 1974, up from 36 percent in 1962. In 1974
women accounted for 18 percent of all managerial and administrators
as compared to 15 percent in 1962. Rapid progress occurred in a
number of higher paying professions, among physicians and surgeons
(6 to 10 percent), and lawyers and judges (3 to 7 percent), in part as a
result of the increased enrollment of women in professional schools.
Women have also made some steady gains in accounting, from 19 to 24
percent; in personnel and labor relations work, from 27 to 35 percent;
in college and university teaching, from 19 to 31 percent; and in
drafting from 4 to 8 percent.[6]

Although the last three decades have seen an extraordinary economic and
social change in the status of women, the employment of women today remains
concentrated in the same industries and occupations in which females have
traditionally worked.[7] Klein states that:

> In 1974, about two-fifths of all women workers 25-54 were employed
> in service industries, one-fifth in manufacturing, another one-fifth in
> trade and the remainder distributed throughout other industries. Fur-
> thermore, within this large age group the under 35 women were some-
> what more likely to be in service industries, and somewhat less likely to
> be in manufacturing and trade than the older women.[8]

A large number of employed older women (55 and over), and younger (24 and
under) also remain employed in service industries.

In terms of occupation, by 1974, "nearly 70 percent of women ages
20 to 24 occupied white collar jobs, but 15 percent had professional and technical jobs and 3 percent occupied managerial and administrative jobs."[9] Sixty
percent of the women in the age group 25 to 54 were white collar workers, but
18 percent occupied professional and technical jobs and 6 percent held managerial and administrative positions.[10] Furthermore, "narrower age distinctions
affect occupational concentrations."[11] In the age group 25 to 34, twenty-three
percent of the women had professional and technical jobs and 4 percent had
managerial and administrative jobs.[12] Fifty-five percent of the women 55 years
and older occupied white collar jobs, but 12 percent had professional and
technical jobs. However, women 55 years and older held more managerial
and administrative jobs (8 percent) as compared with women in the age group
20 to 24 and 25 to 54.[13] This difference, according to McEaddy,[14] is "probably
because of their accumulated years of experience."

The educational achievement of women is an important determinant
of their participation in professional work. About 21 percent of the women
within the age group of 25 to 34 have a college education as compared with
10 percent of the women 55 and over. Among young women 24 and under,
14 percent have a college education.[15]

During the last five years corporations have begun to recruit women with degrees in engineering, data processing, accounting, and business manage-ment. Consequently, there is a tremendous increase in the number of women seeking admission to professional business schools and colleges. In 1967, only 2,505 women were enrolled in engineering schools; in 1972 there were 5,317. The enrollment of females in law schools increased from 3,306 in 1967 to 12,728 in 1972. In terms of total enrollment these five year figures show an increase from 1 percent to 3 percent of the total engineering students, and from 5 percent to 12 percent of the total law students.[16] According to a report on the "Conference of the Redesigning of Work," the enrollment of females in business schools has also increased. At Columbia University 20 percent of the 1973 business class consisted of women as compared with a few female students who had joined the business school a decade before.[17] In 1971, Har-vard Business School graduated 29 women in a class of 754, and the University of Chicago 7 in a class of 280.[18] At the University of Pennsylvania's Wharton School of Business where women averaged less than 4 percent of the student population between 1968 and 1970, women now constitute 25 percent of the present class.[19]

Although women consistently earned less than men in the same age and educational group, the gap between the earnings of men and women tends to be smaller for younger women, particularly among the better educated.[20]

The preceding discussion provides some employment history of women, and the following paragraphs elaborate on women's role in the business world.

Understanding the Changing Role of Women

The traditional role of women as wives and mothers is changing; women are becoming more career-oriented and are entering various business professions. "Women have made inroads into all types of occupations and have assumed jobs ranging from long distance truck drivers to corporate presidents and from bar-tenders to professional football players."[21]

The extraordinarily low birth rate of the 1930's has caused a shortage of males to occupy various management positions in organizations. Further-more during the recession period of the early 1970's a cutback in management training and development was evident. This led to the shortage of well qualified and trained individuals.[22] Considering these factors, it can be concluded "that these are truly auspicious times for women who want careers, responsibility, and challenging work."[23]

Nonetheless, the woman's role in the business world is little under-stood. Some studies have attempted to understand the role of women. In a recent study of one geographical area, it was disclosed that the professional business occupational category having the youngest membership was college teachers and the group having the oldest membership was accountants.[24] It has been suggested that women in management require special training programs because "in general they possess different skills and attitudes toward the managerial role than men."[25] In one study it was found that women are more concerned in their relationships with associates and friends than men.[26] Studies of male and female college students indicate that males are perceived as aggressive, independent, objective, and dominant while females are viewed as tactful, gentle, and quiet.[27] Rosen and Jerdee's study of college undergraduates and bank supervisors demonstrates "that men and women share common perceptions and expectations regarding what constitutes appropriate behavior for males and females in supervisory positions and their attitudes are often influenced by sex-role stereotypes."[28]

Schein reports that:

> successful middle managers are perceived to possess those characteristics, attitudes and temperaments more commonly ascribed to men in general than to women in general. . . . the perceived similarity between the characteristics of successful middle managers and men in general increases the likelihood of a male rather than a female being selected or promoted to a managerial position . . . . and behaviors such as Understanding, Helpful, and Intuitive, are requisite managerial characteristics that are more commonly ascribed to women in general than to men in general.[29]

These findings suggest that "acceptance of stereotypical male characteristics as a basis for success in management may be a necessity for the women seeking to achieve in the current organizational climate."[30]

Although there are certain barriers, i.e., role perception, expectations, male-female stereotypes, and competition which prevent women from moving up the ladder, there is some research evidence which suggests that the differences between men and women are far less important than the similarities between them. In his comparison of female and male leadership styles, Chapman found no significant differences in terms of leadership style between male and female leaders.[31]

Reif, Newstrom, and Monezka's investigation to determine if women managers were psychologically and socially different from men found that:

> (a) psychologically women managers are not significantly different from their male counterparts, and they may possess even superior attributes and skills in some areas related to managerial effectiveness; and (b) from a social psychological standpoint—that is, how they view themselves as a part of the environment within which they operate—the study shows that women managers have much in common with men. Differences do exist, but mostly in ways that would serve to increase the probability of women functioning well as managers.[32]

In an era where women are occupying various managerial positions in all sorts of institutions, it is highly important both from the academic and the organizational point of view that women's motivational strength be studied and analyzed. Since different motives lead to different behavior patterns, it is important that organizations must understand the various needs or motives of its members.

Henry A. Murray (1938) wrote the classic *Explorations in Personality* in which he stated that individuals could be classified according to the strengths of various personality-need variables.[33] These needs were believed to represent a central motivating force, both in terms of the intensity and the direction of goal directed behavior. A need was defined as:

> a construct which stands for a force . . . in the brain region, a force which organizes perception, apperception, intellection, connation, and action in such a way as to transform in a certain direction an existing, unsatisfying situation.[34]

McClelland defined need as "a recurrent concern for a goal state."[35] Murray was concerned with the entire set of needs, and his list included the need for achievement, affiliation, power, autonomy, nurturance, and deference.[36] But McClelland has contributed to the understanding of motivation by centering on three types of basic motivational needs: Need for Achievement (nAch), Need for Affiliation (nAff), and Need for Power (nPow).[37] Since most of the recent research has focused on these three needs, and their relationships to performance in an organizational environment, the following sections will discuss the definitions of the three motives, the measurement of these motives, the methodological considerations, and the objective of this study.

Definition of Motives

Need for Achievement (nAch). Murray defined the need for achievement:

> To accomplish something difficult. To master, manipulate, or organize physical objects, human beings, or ideas. To do this as rapidly and as independently as possible. To overcome obstacles and attain a high standard. To excel one's self. To rival and surpass others. To increase self regard by the successful exercise of talent.[38]

McClelland defines nAch as "behavior toward competition with a standard of excellence."[39] People with a high need for achievement have a great concern to do better, to improve performance, to undertake moderately challenging tasks, to perform better at challenging tasks, to take personal responsibility, and to seek and utilize concrete feed-back on their performance.[40]

Need for Affiliation (nAff). Need for affiliation is defined "as a concern for establishing, maintaining, or restoring a positive affective relationship with another person." Statements expressing a desire to be liked, accepted, or forgiven are manifestations of this motive.[41] People with a high need for affiliation tend to be "approval-seeking, and to select faces rather than neutral stimuli in a perpetual task."[42] They tend to choose friends over experts to work with them on a performance task.[43]

Need for Power (nPow). Need for power is defined as "that disposition, directing behavior toward satisfaction upon the control of the means of influencing another person."[44] People with a high need for power are much concerned with their impact, with their reputation, with their influence, and to accumulate prestige. They try to convince others, and play more competitive sports.[45]

Measurement of Motive Strength

McClelland and his associates have developed a method in which fantasy productions are used to determine the presence and strength of these motives. All three motives are assessed through thematic apperception methods. The Thematic Apperception Test (TAT) is a projective method for the investigation of personality. The TAT consists of a series of pictures about which individuals are instructed to write stories. The thematic pictures are projected onto a screen and time limits are prescribed for completion of stories in response to the pictures. These written stories are examined and coded for their achievement, affiliation, and power imagery.

Four to six pictures are normally used in a group test. A picture is projected for about twenty seconds, then the following four questions are to be answered on prepared forms: (a) What is happening: Who are the persons? (b) What has led up to this situation? That is, what has happened in the past? (c) What is being thought? What is wanted? By whom? (d) What will happen? What will be done?

About one minute is allowed for each question. The individuals are asked to use their imaginations freely in order to tell what the people are thinking and feeling in the story. These stories are then scored for the nAch, nAff, and nPow categories.

Scoring criteria are clearly specified. Instructions and practice materials for learning the method of content analysis enable even an inexperienced coder to attain acceptable interjudge scoring reliability. A detailed discussion of the scoring procedure will be discussed in Chapter III.

Objective of the Study

Various studies (McClelland,[46] Andrews,[47] Cummin,[48] and Wainer and Rubin[49]) have found the three motives (achievement, affiliation, and power) to be related to performance and success in business.

Sex differences play a major role in studying various motives or needs. The problem of measuring the presence and strength of achievement, affiliation, and power motive among women has received some attention, but the available results are inconsistent. Studies aimed at understanding the motivational strength of women managers, especially their need for achievement, affiliation, and power are non-existent.

The objective of this study, therefore, is to determine how strongly women managers are motivated to seek achievement, affiliation, and power, and to what extent these motives are related to their preference for male or female superiors, subordinates, and co-workers. Specific hypotheses related to this objective will be stated in the following paragraphs.

There is no data which can either support or indicate a pattern of need structure among women managers. However, studies have shown similarities in performance between male and female supervisors, and moreover women managers were found to be no different either psychologically or socially from their male counterparts.[50] Consequently, one would expect no significant difference in the need for achievement, affiliation, and power among male and female managers. Studies which have looked into the achievement, affiliation, and power motive of females have either utilized college undergraduate females or women in general. Three studies (Veroff, 1960;[51] Exline, 1960;[52] and Exline, 1962[53]) have found that women in general are more motivated by affiliation than other needs. The recent data on employment and education discussed previously in this chapter reveals that women are getting more education, are seeking professional employment, and that corporations are undertaking extensive searches to locate women managers. It is therefore important to study the motivational characteristics of women managers, because motives are found to be related to performance and other behavioral patterns. It is equally important that an investigation be made to determine if women managers prefer to work for a male or a female boss, and also if they prefer male or female subordinates or co-workers, because the manager's job requires considerable interaction with superiors, subordinates, and co-workers.

These considerations led to the development of the study, and the following null Hypotheses were formulated:

H_1 Women managers when compared with women in general are not significantly different in their need for achievement, affiliation, and power.

H_2 There are no significant differences in their need for achievement, affiliation, and power irrespective of the type of industry in which they are employed, i.e., manufacturing or service sector.

H_3 There are no significant relationships between motives strength and preference for male or female superiors, subordinates, and co-workers.

Furthermore an attempt was made to explore any possible relationship between age, income, education, marital status, managerial experience, and other demographic variables and their need for achievement, affiliation, and power.

The results of this study will contribute to a better understanding of the motivational patterns of women managers. The study has implications for the selection, training, and placement of women managers, as well as yielding information helpful for developing motivational programs especially suited to the female manager.

In this chapter a review of the women's participation in the labor force and education was made. The changing role of women in management and the three motivational concepts which have an important impact on the managerial behavior were also discussed. These considerations led to the formulation of hypotheses. A review of the literature related to this study will be discussed in Chapter II. Chapter III will elaborate on the research methodology. An analysis of data combined with the results will be stated in Chapter IV. And Chapter V will discuss the results, limitations of this research, implications, and suggestions for future research.

NOTES

[1] Edward A. Robie, "Challenge to Management." In Eli Ginzberg and Alice M. Yohalem (Eds.) *Corporate Lib: Women's Challenge to Management,* Baltimore: The Johns Hopkins University Press, 1973, p. 9.

[2] Pearl Meyer, "Women Executives Are Different," *Duns Review,* Jan. 1975, p. 47.

[3] Allyson Sherman Grossman, "Women in the Labor Force: The Early Years." *Monthly Labor Review,* Nov. 1975, p. 3.

[4] Deborah P. Klein, "Women in the Labor Force: The Middle Years." *Monthly Labor Review,* Nov. 1975, p. 10.

[5] Beverly J. McEaddy, "Women in the Labor Force: The Late Years." *Monthly Labor Review,* Nov. 1975, p. 17.

[6] Stuart H. Garfinkle, "Occupation of Women and Black Workers, 1962-74," *Monthly Labor Review,* Nov. 1975, p. 27.

[7] Elizabeth Waldman and Beverly J. McEaddy, "Where Women Work," *Monthly Labor Review,* May, 1974, pp. 3-13.

[8] Klein, *op. cit.* p. 13.

[9] Grossman, *op. cit.* p. 5.

[10] Klein, *op. cit.* p. 14.

[11] *Ibid.,* pp. 13-14.

[12] *Ibid.*

[13] McEaddy, *op. cit.* p. 24.

[14] *Ibid.,* p. 20.

[15] *Ibid.,* p. 21.

[16] John B. Parrish, "Women in Professional Training." *Monthly Labor Review,* May, 1974, p. 421.

[17] "Women's Work Has Just Begun:" Report on the Conference on the Redesigning of Work. The Newschool, New York: September 17, 1973.

[18] Robie, *op. cit.* p. 22.

[19] "Up the Ladder, Finally," *Business Week,* Nov., 1975, p. 62.

[20] Klein, *op. cit.* p. 14.

[21] Lena B. Prewitt, "The Employment Rights of the Female." Speech delivered at the Personnel Meeting of the Southeastern Electric Exchange. Baton Rouge, La: October 4, 1973.

[22] M.V. Higginson and T.L. Quick, *The Ambitious Women's Guide to a Successful Career.* AMA Com., 1975, pp. 3-4.

[23] *Ibid.*

[24] Rose E. Knotts, "Manifest Needs of Professional Female Workers in Business-Related Occupations." *Journal of Business Research.* 1975, 3, pp. 267-276.

[25] Marshall H. Brenner, "Management Development for Women," *Personnel Journal.* March, 1972, p. 166.

[26] Edgar S. Ellman, *Managing Women in Business.* National Foreman's Institute, Bureau of Business Practice, National Sales Development Institute. Water, Conn: 1963, p. 23.

[27] P. Rosenkratz, et. al., "Sex-Role Stereotypes and Self-Concepts in College Students." *Journal of Consulting and Clinical Psychology.* 1968, 32, pp. 287-295.

[28] B. Rosen and T.H. Jerdee, "The Influence of Sex-Role Stereotypes on Evaluation of Male and Female Supervisory Behavior." *Journal of Applied Psychology.* 1973, 57, p. 47.

[29] V. Schein, "The Relationship between Sex-Role Stereotypes and Requisite Management Characteristics." *Journal of Applied Psychology,* 1973, 57, p. 99.

[30] V.E. Schein, "Relationship between Sex-Role Stereotypes and Requisite Management Characteristics Among Female Managers." *Journal of Applied Psychology,* 1975, 60, p. 343.

[31] J.B. Chapman, "Comparison of Male and Female Leadership Styles." *Academy of Management Journal,* 1975, 18, pp. 645-650.

[32] William E. Reif, et. al., "Exploding Some Myths About Women Managers." *California Management Review,* 1975, 17, p. 78.

[33] H.A. Murray, *Explorations in Personality,* New York: Oxford University Press, 1938.

[34] *Ibid.,* p. 123.

[35] David C. McClelland, *Assessing Human Motivation.* New York: General Learning Press, 1971, p. 13.

[36] Murray, *op. cit.* pp. 82-83.

[37] David C. McClelland, et al., *The Achievement Motive.* New York: Appleton-Century-Crofts, 1953.

[38] Murray, *op. cit.,* p. 124.

[39] McClelland, *The Achievement Motive, op. cit.,* p. 110.

[40] David C. McClelland, "Business Drive and National Achievement." *Harvard Business Review.* July-August, 1962, pp. 99-112.

[41] Roger W. Heyns, et al., "A Scoring Manual for the Affiliation Motive." In J.A. Atkinson (Ed.) *Motives in Fantasy, Action, and Society.* Princeton, N.J.: Van Nostrand, 1958, p. 205.

[42] J.W. Atkinson and E.L. Walker, "The Affiliation Motive and Perceptual Sensitivity to Faces." *Journal of Abnormal and Social Psychology,* 1956, 53, pp. 38-41.

[43] E.G. French, "Motivation as a Variable in Work Partner Selection." *Journal of Abnormal and Social Psychology,* 1956, 53, pp. 96-99.

[44] Joseph Veroff, "Development and Validation of a Projective Measure of Power Motivation." In J.W. Atkinson (Ed.) *Motives in Fantasy, Action, and Society.* Princeton: Van Nostrand, 1958, p. 105.

[45] David G. Winter, *The Power Motive.* New York: The Free Press: Collier MacMillan Publishers, 1973.

[46] David C. McClelland, *The Achieving Society.* Princeton: Van Nostrand, 1961.

[47] J. Andrews, "The Achievement Motive in Two Types of Organization,"*Journal of Personality and Social Psychology,* 1967, 6, pp. 163-168.

[48] P.C. Cummin, "TAT Correlates of Executive Performance." *Journal of Applied Psychology,* 1967, 51, pp. 78-81.

[49] H.A. Wainer and I.M. Rubin, "Motivation of Research and Development Entrepreneurs. Determinants of Company Success." *Journal of Applied Psychology,* 1969, 53, pp. 178-184.

[50] Reif, et al., *op. cit.,* p. 78.

[51] Joseph Veroff, et al., "The Use of Thematic Apperception to Assess Motivation in a Nationwide Interview Study." *Psychological Monographs,* 1960, 94, (12, Whole No. 499).

[52] R.V. Exline, "Effect of Sex, Norms, and Affiliation upon Accuracy of Perception of Interpersonal Preference." *Journal of Personality,* 1960, 28, pp. 397-412.

[53] R.V. Exline, "Need Affiliation and Initial Communication Behavior in Problem Solving Groups Characterized by Low Interpersonal Visibility." *Psychological Reports,* 1962, 10, pp. 79-89.

CHAPTER II

GENERAL BACKGROUND THEORY AND RESEARCH

The chapter discusses the theoretical and research background as it relates to achievement, affiliation, and power motivation.

Much of the work done in this area is found in the psychology or sociology literature; however, related work appearing in management literature is quite fragmented. The purpose of this chapter, therefore, is to integrate such sections of the literature which are relevant and appropriate in the field of management.

The chapter is divided into three sections which will elaborate on the origin and development of each of the three motives in general and as it relates to women, and will identify various features of behavior associated with these motives. Some of the studies reported in this chapter are focused on male subjects; therefore, care must be taken when generalizing the findings to include women.

Achievement Motivation: Origin and Development

McClelland and his co-workers presented a projective measure of nAch, defined as "concern with success in competition with some standards of excellence."[1] In addition, they presented a number of studies to establish the construct validity of the measure. The strength of motivation was first demonstrated with hunger. To determine the effect of hunger on thematic apperception stories, McClelland and Atkinson conducted an experiment on Navy personnel. The sailors were deprived of food for varying periods. Analysis of stories indicated a positive relationship between hunger and motivation. This experiment demonstrated that the hungry (motivated) sailors wrote stories about hungry (motivated) people.[2]

Individual motivation can be analyzed by utilizing content analysis of one's fantasy or imaginative behavior. The work of McClelland (1961), Atkinson (1964), Atkinson and Feather (1966) and Atkinson (1974) have provided still more research and theory about individual motives.[3, 4, 5, 6] The strengths and differences in achievement motivation among individuals have been found as early as the age of five, and the achievement motive remains quite stable from this age through adulthood.[7] This indicates that achievement motive is developed at an early age, and it appears to depend to a large extent on the child's training in independence. Winterbottom's research determined that the amount, timing, and type of independence that a young child received (training, etc.) has the greatest impact on his or her later drive for achievement.[8] She found that mothers of boys with high need for achievement demanded more independence and mastery at an earlier age than mothers of boys with low need for achievement. By setting high standards for them, the mothers expected the children to be self-reliant, make their own friends, do well in competition, entertain themselves, and earn their own money at a significantly younger age than mothers of low achievers. On the other hand, mothers of sons with a low need for achievement tended to restrict their son's activities and discourage their decision making capability by making them dependent on parents. In a similar study Rosen and D'Andrade also found that mothers and fathers of the boys with high need for achievement established high standards of excellence and gave more responsiblity to their children than parents of the boys with low need for achievement.[9] Also important is the fact that a child should exercise his or her own behavior without being controlled by his father.[10] Therefore, the principal psychological factor in the development of achievement motivation is the attitude of the parents. The role of the mother and the father in developing independence, mastery, and setting high standards is very important; however, this should "occur neither too early for the child's abilities, nor too late for him or (her) to internalize these standards as his or (her) own."[11]

An over-all conclusion based on the foregoing research is that "The relatively demanding parent who clearly instigates self-reliance in the child and who then rewards independent behavior is teaching the child a need for achievement."[12] These differences in child rearing seem to be reflected in work habits.

As a result of child rearing practices, achievement motivated people are more likely to be found in certain groups or classes of society than in others. Societies which have more achievement motivated individuals experience a rapid economic growth and prosperity, whereas a society consisting of low achievers will experience a decline in the economy. McClelland supported this conclusion by analyzing the achievement content in the children's readers from about 30 countries.[13] The achievement scores from the children's readers were related to indices of economic development. The results showed that a concern for achievement as expressed in imaginative literature—folk tales and stories for children—was associated with a more rapid rate of economic development. This relationship was confirmed not only for Western democracies like England and the United States, but also for communist countries like Russia, Bulgaria, and Hungary. In a similar study DeCharms and Moeller reported a positive relationship between achievement content in children's readers and economic development of the United States.[14]

Individuals with high need for achievement prefer not to take high risks.[15] They avoid "sure thing" by setting goals that require some individual effort and challenge on their part, but avoid goals over which they have little control.[16] Accordingly they prefer to work on tasks with moderate risk. Meyer, Walker and Litwin reported that the managers with high need for achievement at General Electric preferred moderate over high or low risks.[17] This indicates that managers with high need for achievement are more realistic in setting of goals than managers with low need for achievement.

Various studies have reported a relationship between performance and achievement motivation. People who score high in nAch do extremely better in school and college, and learn faster than those with low nAch scores.[18, 19, 20, 21] Furthermore, high achievers set moderate goals, perform better in school, and attain a higher level of education.[22]

Achievement motivation is also related to academic background and occupational choice. In general, adults (male and female) with a university education have a stronger achievement motive and also are more apt to occupy professional positions than low achieving adults.[23] This implies that individuals with high nAch prefer to engage in tasks which are interesting and challenging to them. Therefore, achievement motivated individuals are more often found in business careers, particularly in sales and marketing. These careers offer challenge and opportunity to take risks with explicit knowledge of results (i.e., profits and losses). McClelland's study of executives in four countries (United States, Italy, Turkey, and Poland) reported that the average nAch score for marketing managers from the four countries was relatively higher when compared with other business functions, i.e., general management, finance, engineering, and personnel. [24] In a subsequent study, McClelland analyzed achievement scores of college sophomores and eleven years later compared their scores with occupational choice. The results indicated that among those who were classified as holding entrepreneurial occupations, 83 percent scored high in achievement motive.[25] This indicates that high achievers possess many of the characteristics of the ambitious businessman. Entrepreneurs are primarily driven by the achievement motive and are interested in profits because it serves as feedback and a measure of their competence and performance.[26] Need for achievement is also found to be related to managerial success,[27] especially in the sales area.[28]

According to Bass and Barrett:

> The individuals with high achievement motivation work longer and probably harder than others, but only at tasks which will give them some feeling of accomplishment. If the task is too easy or routine, they will do no better than those with a low need for achievement. Individuals with high need for achievement will work just as hard for a group goal as for an individual goal to the extent that the task is challenging and provides a feeling of accomplishment.[29]

Various studies by French,[30] French and Thomas,[31] and Mehrabian[32] indicated that people with a high nAch are more likely to work on a problem for a longer period of time and are more likely to reach a solution; however, they may not do well at tasks which are boring, routine, and offer no challenge.

Individuals high in achievement motivation select achievement oriented tasks and take personal responsibility for the success or failure of the task.[33]

It has also been shown that "executives high in nAch tend to have less meetings than other executives and tend to want to work alone, despite the fact that many organizational problems would be better solved by collaborative effort."[34] This means that high nAch individuals are strongly concerned with competition and might be described as task-oriented.

Selection of work partners is also related to achievement motivation. French, in distinguishing behavior in performance of tasks of those high in achievement motivation and those who showed strong affiliation motivation, reported that when people with high nAch were asked to select a partner to help them perform a task, they selected partners who were competent rather than friends. People with a low nAch but high nAff selected friends rather than competent work partners.[35] Job preference, structure, rewards, and organizational factors are also related to achievement motive. In a nation-wide study, Veroff et al. found managers to be among those who have the highest need for achievement and achievement scores were significantly higher for individuals holding high-status occupations.[36] In a study of two groups of managers and specialists in a large industrial organization, managers were found to have a significantly stronger need for achievement than specialists.[37] In McClelland's study of need achievement of executives and professionals in four countries (United States, Italy, Turkey, and Poland) managers were found to be higher than the professionals in their need for achievement in every country except Turkey.[38]

In a laboratory study designed to investigate the effectiveness of leadership style with different levels of nAch, Misumi and Seki found that high nAch individuals performed better under leaders who were task as well as people oriented, whereas individuals with low nAch performed better only under task oriented leaders.[39] This indicates that an environment which provides some degree of personal responsibility, control and performance feedback is most appropriate for individuals motivated to achieve. This is consistent with other empirical studies which report that: "people with high need for achievement prefer jobs which allow them more personal responsibility for their behavior and its consequences."[40] They also want considerable structure in their work setting and utilize structure to receive feedback so that they can be confident of reward for excellent performance.[41] According to Litwin, "rewards for an excellent performance and 'fair appraisal' of all performance stimulates individuals high in nAch to strive for these rewards as symbols of their success and personal achievement."[42] Furthermore, "high achievers expect to be rewarded for a positive performance and to be punished for a negative performance to a much greater degree than men with a low need for achievement."[43]

The close relationship between achievement motivation and success in managerial activities continues to be documented by specialists in this field. McClelland looks to the entrepreneur as the one who translates nAch into economic development.[44] Schrage's study of R & D entrepreneurs indicates that the profitable companies are run by individuals who have a high need for achievement.[45] Wainer and Rubin's study of a technically based firm in the Boston area also found high need for achievement to be positively related to company performance.[46] However, "those who scored low in nAch were not significantly lower performers than those whose nAch was moderate.[47] Studies of executives of two Mexican firms also demonstrated that the top executives of the achievement firms were higher in need for achievement than power. An individual's need for achievement and advancement was found to be positively related.[48] In another study, company success was found to be related to the high achievement scores of the businessmen.[49]

Achievement Motivation in Women

The very few studies dealing with the achievement motivation of females have not produced any consistent data. "Perhaps the most persistent unresolved problem in research on achievement concerns the observed sex differences."[50]

Crandall and his associates have offered some explanation as to what accounts for the difference in the achievement behavior between boys and girls. Boys are conditioned to aspire because of the social acceptability attached to success.[51] On the other hand, girls may be rewarded simply for trying or conversely may even be criticized for "stating high (though realistic) expectations and standards as unfeminine boasting."[52] In this culture achievement is considered a part of the male role.[53] Such attitudes have important implications for intellectual development of girls at later ages.[54]

Kagan and Moss reported that criticism of girls by mothers in their early years was associated with high independence and high achievement later on. They also reported that girls are encouraged to be dependent and boys are trained to be aggressive.[55] In comparing the attitudes of parents of high achievers with low achievers, it was reported that mothers of underachieving girls "encouraged dependency, appeared to be more dominant, and did not tolerate the aggressive behavior of their children."[56] Similar results were found by Teahan.[57]

Lesser, in discussing the two studies of Pierce (1961) and Stivers (1965) report that:

> High school girls with high need achievement scores are less likely to seek additional formal school, are more likely to get a job immediately or get married after high school. Girls who are highly motivated to achieve are more likely to go into the adult world upon high school

graduation than to college. This suggests that achievement in high school girls attaches itself not to academic performance (as it does in boys), but rather to the more immediate adult goals.[58]

In an attempt to determine if there were any substantial differences in achievement motivation among various female groups with a college education, Baruch found "that the achievement motivation was strongest among women who were in their fifth year after college graduation."[59] Low achievement among older groups was attributed to various household responsibilities taken by the older women.

In a nationwide study of males and females, Veroff and his associates report that: women with high need for achievement were college educated and came from small towns and rural areas. The highest motivation was found in the age (55-64) group followed by the age (25-44) group.[60]

Although the EPPS (Edwards Personal Preference Schedule) is not correlated with TAT, studies by Knotts,[61] Anderson and McDowell[62] using EPPS indicate that professional females and MBA female students have a greater need for achievement and dominance, and a lower need for affiliation. Similar results on females were reported by Jacobs and Podhoretz.[63,64]

The occupation and education of parents also have some bearing on the achievement motivation of females. In one study, need for achievement among high school girls was found to be associated with the father's education and occupation,[65] while another study reported that mothers make an important contribution in developing the achievement motive among girls. The mother's occupational status was also identified as one determinant of achievement motivation in girls.[66]

According to Vernon:

the appearance and causes of achievement motivation in men and women vary considerably. Marked achievement in women may result in social disapproval and therefore, they may show achievement oriented behavior only in a friendly social surrounding.[67]

This suggests that the female pattern of achievement motivation is markedly different from that of men. Similar viewpoint is expressed by Stein and Bailey:

one of the most important areas for female achievement is social skill. Achievement striving and social activity are more closely linked for females than for males. This link has frequently been interpreted as indicating that females' achievement striving is motivated by need for affiliation or external social approval rather than by an internalized desire to meet a standard of excellence. . . . Instead, it appears that attainment of excellence is often a goal of females' achievement efforts, but the areas in which attainment is sought are frequently social skills and other areas perceived as feminine.[68]

The very few studies which have reported data on achievement motivation among women have consisted of either college students or women in general. They may not relate well to today's women in management.

The role of women has changed considerably over the last few years. Various employment and educational data along with studies aimed at learning the attitudes of women managers discussed previously indicate that: more women are acquiring college education; the enrollment of women in professional schools has been increasing steadily; executive recruiters are constantly searching for women executives; women are trying to adjust in the traditionally male dominated world; and finally, women managers have more similarities than dissimilarities when compared with male managers.

In spite of the similarities between male and female managers, studies to measure the motives of women managers may quite possibly produce a different set of data which may be of importance.

Affiliation Motivation: Origin and Development

The concept of affiliation motive relates to a person's concern about the quality of his personal relationships. The affiliation motive was originally developed by Shipley and Veroff, and various studies have shown why people have a need to affiliate.[69] Harlow's research on monkeys indicates an innate need for social contact.[70]

> Some form of social contact appears necessary for the normal physical and personality development of the human infant; and total isolation is virtually always an intolerable situation for the human adult—even when physical needs are provided for.[71]

This suggests that social need exists among most adult human beings. In terms of dependency, it appears that there are differences between men and women. In this culture dependency for a male is less acceptable than dependency for a female. There is some indication that the parents of affiliation motivated children emphasize close family ties, and dependency during childhood. Schachter's study of co-eds demonstrated that co-eds who wanted to affiliate were the first born child in the family or were the only child.[72] This finding implies that earlier born children have a greater opportunity to learn to be dependent on their parents, whereas later-born children have less tendency to be dependent on their parents.

In his well-known study of co-eds Schachter demonstrated that increasing anxiety tended to increase affiliation motivation. Two groups of co-eds were subjected to two different conditions. One group (high anxiety group) was told that the shock would be administered, while the second group (low anxiety condition) was told that the shock would be mild. Ultimately no shocks were administered. The objective was to determine whether the two groups wanted to be together or alone when frightened. The results showed that most of the subjects in the high-anxiety group preferred to wait with the others while most of those in the low-anxiety group did not care one way or the other. In other words, anxiety increased the need for affiliation.[73] Thus people need to affiliate with others, but affiliation is more desirable when people are similar in some important ways. In many instances, people seek affiliation because they desire to have their beliefs confirmed. Literature from sociology also indicates that people tend to group together during a crisis.

A comprehensive work on affiliative behavior by Crowne and Marlowe suggests that:

> the goal or need of the approval seeking person includes social recognition, status protection, dependency, love, and affection. They have learned that submission, and conformity entail the fewer risks of social recognition and threats to self-esteem. . . . Furthermore, approval seeking individuals agree with the judgment of the group, and seldom exercise independent judgments.[74]

The relationship between affiliation motive and conformity is not very clear. Individuals motivated to affiliate conform to get acceptance, respect, and status from members of the social group to which they belong, "because their status in society is partly determined by the positions they occupy, and the role they play in these groups."[75] Although research evidence on whether affiliation motive leads to conformity is not conclusive, one study reported that when pressure is applied by a friend to do something, people with a high need for affiliation motive are more likely to comply than people with a low need for affiliation.[76] However, it cannot be implied that people with a high need for affiliation will conform to all group pressures. The decision to conform or not to conform depends on a number of other motivational forces.[77] The "acquiescent" individual may be easily influenced by any social pressure, but the independent individual may agree only when his interests are compatible with the interest of the group.[78]

Affiliation motivation and achievement are quite different from each other. People motivated to affiliate are concerned with the establishment and maintenance of affectionate relationships with others. Whereas the need for affiliation governs the interpersonal relationship, the need for achievement is an individualized need.

> A person motivated mainly by achievement motivation may make important contributions to society, but may not be the most comfortable person to live with . . . he works hard when he gets involved in a problem, whereas a person motivated primarily by affiliation may not be so involved in getting the job done, because people mean more to him than the task.[79]

One study compared the task performance of achievement and affiliation motivated individuals under two different conditions. The results showed that subjects high in need for achievement worked more efficiently in the "task feedback" situation. The reverse was true of the subjects high in need for affiliation. They worked well in the "feeling feedback" situation and did not do so well with "task feedback."[80] This suggests that people with a high need for affiliation react favorably to information concerning the human aspects as compared to the information concerning the task. Furthermore the climate in the two groups was quite different. People motivated to achieve argued violently and were anxious to complete the task whereas people with affiliation motive showed friendly interest and were quiet. In another study, it was found that when people with high affiliation and low achievement motive were asked to select a partner to help them perform a task, they selected partners who were friends even though the partner was rather incompetent. The opposite was true for people with high achievement motive.[81] Similar results were reported by Rosenfield.[82]

Whyte in his book *The Organization Man* states that people conform and readily accept organizational policies and ideas and therefore do not submit their own ideas or opinions because they want to fit in with the organization to which they belong.[83] Other studies have found the affiliation motive to be related to "approval-seeking behavior" and opinion change, especially when they like the other person.[84, 85] This implies that nAff is stronger than nAch in such executives. Yet, McClelland's study of managers and professionals indicates that U.S. managers have a higher need for achievement than affiliation.[86] An analysis of other studies done by Meyer, Walker, and Litwin,[87] Wainer and Rubin,[88] Andrews,[89] and Cummins[90] does not provide any support to Whyte's argument. Whyte's argument, however, may be true in organizations with a bureaucratic environment. Such organizations have relatively little room for improvement and innovation, and consequently there is little challenge. Organizations which are competitive in nature are quite concerned with new ideas and tend to hire specialists, and provide challenge and responsibility in their jobs. This suggests that achievement oriented people join organizations which provide challenge, while people motivated primarily by affiliation join organizations where there is less challenge but where affiliation is rewarded.

The need for affiliation and individual task performance are not, however, unrelated. A study of undergraduate students to determine the relationship between the strength of the affiliation motive and cooperation found the productivity of high nAff individuals to be high in cooperative task group.[91]

From a managerial viewpoint, the maintenance of effective interpersonal relationships with workers is a very important aspect of the manager's job. Too much concern for the people, however, may create problems for the manager. When confronted with the problem of meeting performance goals, he (or she) may not be willing to disrupt his (or her) relationship by being forthright, and thus becomes less productive.[92] Such a relationship (the goal of maintaining friendly relations) "supersedes a concern over the effectiveness of his (or her) organizational unit's performance toward corporate objectives."[93]

One study has shown positive relationship between affiliation motive and performance. Lawrence and Lorsch studied the motives of twenty managers who were responsible for integrating the work of various units or people. They found that effective integrators had higher need for affiliation than the less effective integrators. "The effective integrators paid more attention to others and their feelings, worked hard to maintain friendly relationships in meetings, and accepted assignments which offered opportunities for interaction."[94] This finding is important because a manager's job "requires him (or her) to develop people and their skills so that they can perform better."[95]

The research on affiliation motive discussed in this chapter indicates that people have a need to seek approval, recognition, confirm their beliefs, reduce anxiety, and maintain friendly relationships. However, high affiliation need as reported in various studies causes some degree of conflict in organizational goals, when task orientation conflicts with the need to affiliate.

Affiliation Motivation in Women

The limited data available on women indicate that they have a high need for affiliation. Two studies of college students reported that affiliation scores for females were significantly higher than males.[96, 97] Veroff's study also reported high affiliation need among women in general. The study also reported that educated women were higher in affiliation than less educated. Younger and middle aged women had higher need for affiliation than older women. Women with high need for affiliation lived in metropolitan areas and came from broken families (parents divorced or separated).[98] The research data on affiliation motive among women, however, is limited and therefore cannot be generalized. In the absence of any data on women managers, it is difficult to make any predictions.

Power Motivation: Origin and Development

The word "power" is not one of the best-liked or even most understood words. In his conversation with Dowling, Warren Bennis states that:

> If you think about the Victorian era, Freud and right through Blooms-bury, the liberated crowd in England, it was a period in which sex was a dominant issue expressed clearly either in its suppression or its celebration. By now it's easier for people to talk about sex on talk shows than to talk of finances. Finances are the next thing that will come into the open, as we become more of a public-sector society. Power is

the last of the little dirty secrets. People who have it don't want to talk about it; people who don't have it don't want to talk about it. You know there are books called *The Sensual Woman, The Sensual Man, The Sensual Couple.* When we start seeing books on the powerful man, the powerful woman, the powerful couple, we'll know that this problem is no longer tucked away. There will be an occasional article called "Power: A Neglected Variable," and it will tell how we haven't discussed power—period.[99]

The word power is derived from the Old Latin *potere* meaning "to be able"[100] and is defined in the general sense as the "ability or official capacity to exercise control, authority."[101] Individuals who study power have used different definitions which fit the type of power they are examining. Winter defines "social power" as "the ability or capacity to control the behavior or emotions of another person."[102] Adler meant "the ability to manipulate or control the activities of others to suit one's own purposes."[103] Most definitions seem to have the terms "ability" and "control" in common whether power is directed at objects, persons, or behavior. These and other definitions lead to power as a broad concept which may be enlarged or looked at from different perspectives.

Weber analyzed power according to how it was perceived by followers. He outlines three ways of power to be legitimized: "rational-legal authority, traditional authority, or charismatic influence."[104] French and Raven defined five different areas of power: "reward, coercive, legitimate, referent, and expert."[105] The concept of Machiavellian power, which to some has "bad" connotations, shows the following characteristics: "willingness to manipulate others, a lack of concern for conventional morality, a willingness to exploit others in pursuit of personal goals, and emotional detachment in inter-personal situations."[106] It has also been studied from a position standpoint where power is derived from an organizational job and from a personal standpoint where personality is the source.[107]

Winter stresses the rather complex idea of the power motive, which he defines as:

> a disposition to strive for certain kind of goals, or to be affected by certain kind of incentives. People who have the power motive are trying to bring about a certain state of affairs. They want to feel power and power is their goal.[108]

However, to simply state that someone is powerful is not meaningful. The question of why someone possesses power and how to predict those who do or do not have power would be very useful and lend more meaning to the concept.

Individuals actively engaged in attempts to acquire power show two characteristics of interpersonal style. First, they strive to become known or gain visibility. In doing this, they speak of change by attacking the establishment, using their own ideology which presumably comes from a source having great worth. Second, they build an organization, often recruiting the poor or destitute who have little to lose by choosing to follow. This tactic insures that the leader remains independent of the establishment and enhances his chance of gaining a power base.[109] For people high in power motive the satisfaction of gaining recognition from their fellow men is more important than for people with a low need for power.[110] High nPow individuals seek rank and status as personal goals and will form alliances as a means of reaching those goals, and once reached, they tend to spend money on possessions which reflect prestige.[111]

In order to convince or influence other people, power motivated individuals are argumentative, confronting, and they like personal recognition and approval because it legitimizes the goals of power and thus increases the salience of power motive syndrome.[112] According to Litwin and Stringer this means that:

> organizational climates characterized by confrontation and tolerance for conflict will arouse power motive only when the person feels that he is a regular, long term member of the organization; and when his status and influence are related to his ability to deal with and confront conflict.[113]

In a study of MBA students and managers, it was found that power motivated individuals "preferred considerable structure in their work environment because they perceive structure as providing a clear understanding of responsibility and power."[114] Although both achievement and power motivated individuals prefer considerable structure in their work environment, the reasons are quite different. Whereas a person with a high need for achievement "wants structure to receive performance feedback, a person with a high need for power wants structure for status."[115]

Studies conducted at Wesleyan and Harvard Universities on male undergraduate students have shown that individuals high on nPow tend to seek formal social power by occupying offices where there is real power. They participate in sports which are highly competitive such as football, tennis, and baseball. Their political ambitions involve seeking election to offices which are high in the expectancy of power.[116]

Winter's study also provides some data on occupational and career selections. Individuals with strong power needs tend to be attracted to occupations which afford them considerable scope in defining their roles, selecting their actions, advising and helping others, and controlling and evaluating the behavior of others. Careers in teaching, psychology, and business management ranked at the top of chosen careers by individuals with high need for power, whereas careers in law, medicine, and civil service ranked at the bottom.[117] This is consistent with the data obtained from a longitudinal study of graduates from Oxford, England.[118] Careers selected by the graduates were compared with the power scores obtained later on. It was found that high nPow graduates had selected careers in teaching and business management. Veroff and his associates also found managers to have the strongest need for power.[119]

Past thinking has equated success with high need for achievement. Recent studies indicate that the power motive is also related to managerial success. Since managers are primarily concerned with directing and coordinating the activities of the organization, and are less concerned with innovations and improvements, it seems obvious that "they should be characterized by a high need for power," because any kind of coordination and control requires influence.[120]

In another study, the need for power was measured for middle and upper level managers who worked in a number of different business organizations. The executives were classified into high and low success groups on the basis of how their salaries compared to the salaries of other executives of comparable age. It was found that the most successful executives scored significantly higher in the need for power than did the less successful executives. It was concluded that successful executives show a definite desire for "increased responsibility and control under the organizational hierarchy."[121] Yet, in a study of Mexican Businessmen nPow was found to be negatively related to advancement in the achievement oriented firm (dynamic organization), and positively related to advancement in the power oriented firm (non-progressive). Furthermore, the power oriented firm emphasized dominance and dependence.[122] The study indicates that power motivated individuals find it easy to progress in a power oriented environment. On the other hand, high need for power may be a detriment for advancing in the achievement oriented firms. High need for power was found to be unrelated to the performance of entrepreneurs. However, the successful entrepreneurs had high need for achievement and a moderate need for power.[123] This means that the entrepreneurs' motive profile is different than that of managers. McClelland also pointed out that entrepreneurs must be distinguished from managers. Entrepreneurs are innovative and are also concerned with improvements and long range planning; therefore, they should exhibit a higher need for achievement than power.[124] A recent study of corporate executives presents a new behavioral pattern. It indicates that individuals high in nPow, low in nAff, and high in inhibition (Institutional Managers) have more propensity for success in business careers. Need for power must "be disciplined and controlled so that it is directed towards the benefit of the institution as a whole and not towards the manager's personal aggrandizement."[125] These findings, therefore, place emphasis on personal maturity, the proper use of control regarding power, and overall concern for organizational goals as opposed to personal ones.

High need for power does not guarantee success. Individuals with high power motive may place too much emphasis on control and ignore giving assistance and guidance to others. If these individuals are also low in nAff, then the tendency to become outspoken and impatient may lead to a dictatorial attitude.

Power Motivation in Women

The subject of female or male dominance historically follows a cyclical pattern, rising and falling over a period of time. Today women enjoy many of the freedoms for which they have campaigned through the years. Education is now fairly equal, and birth control measures are used with increasing frequency, thereby freeing women from unwanted pregnancies.[126]

There are three commonly held beliefs concerning the relationship between power and sex:

> First, that men are more interested in getting power than women; second, that men and women differ in the ways they establish, maintain, and express power; and third, that sex involves domination, power, and exploitation.[127]

Research data on power motive in women challenge all of these beliefs. It has been reported that women and men are equally interested in getting power. Fourteen studies found no significant differences in power motive among the two sexes. These studies on men and women were conducted under similar conditions using TAT pictures.[128]

Men seek and get formal social power by holding office and membership in voluntary organizations. They tend to enter careers which give them power to direct others' behavior. The available data show that women exhibit the same type of behavior both as to office holding and career choice. In a sample of 70 women from a New England private college, considering those women who planned any full time career, the power motive predicted the same careers for females as those planned by power motivated men.[129]

Veroff in his nation wide study found: college educated women to have more power than non-college educated women; younger women in the age group (21-34) scored higher in power motivation than older women; women with high nPow came from metropolitan areas; and married women tend to have higher need for power than widows.[130]

In one study the consumption of alcohol among adult women has also been found to be related to power motive.[131] However, Stewart and Winter in their studies of college women found no relationship between power and consumption of alcohol.[132]

Winter summarizes the research on the power motive in women. The available data support three conclusions which are at variance with traditional beliefs:

Women are as interested in power as men; when interested in power or motivated for power, women are as instrumental about getting formal social power as are men; and power motivated women do not view sex as a form of power, unlike their male counterparts, therefore, they have no special problems dealing with the opposite sex.[133]

The literature on achievement, affiliation, and power motive related to this study indicates that women in general tend to have high need for affiliation. There is some evidence that educated women tend to show a greater need for achievement than less educated women. The data on power motivation tend to suggest that men and women do not differ significantly in terms of their need for power. Again it must be noted that the available data are based on studies conducted on either college women or women in general. It is, therefore, difficult to draw any conclusions as to what kind of behaviors or needs women managers will show in this study.

A review of the literature on achievement, affiliation, and power motive was covered in this chapter. Chapter III will discuss the research methodology employed in this study.

NOTES

[1] David C. McClelland, et al., *The Achievement Motive*. New York: Appleton-Century-Crofts, 1953, p. 110.

[2] D.C. McClelland and J.W. Atkinson, "The Effect of Different Intensities of the Hunger Drive on Thematic Apperception." In J.W. Atkinson (Ed.) *Motives in Fantasy, Action, and Society*. Princeton: Van Nostrand, 1958, pp. 46-63.

[3] D.C. McClelland, *The Achieving Society*. Princeton: Van Nostrand, 1961.

[4] J.W. Atkinson, *An Introduction to Motivation*. Princeton: Van Nostrand, 1964.

[5] J.W. Atkinson and N.T. Feather, *A Theory of Achievement Motivation*. New York: John Wiley and Sons, 1966.

[6] J.W. Atkinson and J.O. Raynor (Eds.) *Motivation and Achievement*. Washington, D.C.: V.H. Winston (Distributed by Halsted Press of John Wiley & Co.), 1974.

[7] J. Kagan and H.A. Moss, *Birth to Maturity*. New York: John Wiley and Sons, 1962.

[8] M.R. Winterbottom, "The Relations of Need for Achievement to Learning Experience in Independence and Mastery." In J.W. Atkinson (Ed.) *Motives in Fantasy, Action, and Society*. Princeton: Van Nostrand, 1958, pp. 453-478.

[9] B.C. Rosen and R.G. D'Andrade, "The Psychological Origins of Achievement Motivation." *Sociometry*, 1959, 22. pp. 185-218.

[10] F.L. Strodtbeck, "Family Interaction Values and Achievement." In D.C. McClelland, et al., *Talent and Society*, Princeton: Van Nostrand, 1958, pp. 135-194.

[11] McClelland, *The Achieving Society, op. cit.*, p. 345.

[12] F.H. Sanford and L.S. Wrightsman. *Psychology*. Belmont, California: Brooks-Cole, 1970, p. 212.

[13] McClelland, *The Achieving Society, op. cit.*, pp. 70-105.

[14] R. DeCharms and G.H. Moeller, "Values Expressed in American Children's Readers." *Journal of Abnormal and Social Psychology*, 1962, 64, pp. 136-142.

[15] David C. McClelland, "Business Drive and National Achievement." *Harvard Business Review*, July-August, 1962, pp. 99-112.

[16] J.W. Atkinson, "Motivational Determinants of Risk Taking Behavior." In J.W. Atkinson and N.T. Feather. (Eds.) *A Theory of Achievement Motivation*. New York: John Wiley and Sons, 1966, pp. 11-30.

[17] H.H. Meyer, W.B. Walker and G.H. Litwin, "Motive Patterns and Risk Preferences Associated with Entrepreneurship." *Journal of Abnormal and Social Psychology*, 1961, 63, pp. 570-574.

[18] J.W. Atkinson and W.R. Reitman, "Performance as a Function of Motive Strength and Expectance of Goal Attainment." *Journal of Abnormal and Social Psychology*, 1956, 53, pp. 361-366.

[19] McClelland, et al., *The Achievement Motive, op. cit.,* pp. 237-238.

[20] R.A. Clark and D.C. McClelland, "A Factor Analytical Integration of Imaginative and Performance Measures of the Need for Achievement." *Journal of General Psychology,* 1956, 55, pp. 73-83.

[21] E.L. Lowell, "The Effect of Need for Achievement on Learning and Speed of Performance." *Journal of Psychology,* 1952, 33, pp. 31-40.

[22] H.J. Crockett, "The Achievement Motive and Differential Occupational Mobility in the United States." *American Sociological Review,* 1962, 27, pp. 191-204.

[23] Joseph Veroff, et al., "The Use of Thematic Apperception to Assess Motivation in a Nationwide Interview Study." *Psychological Monographs,* 1960, 94 (12, Whole No. 499).

[24] McClelland, *The Achieving Society, op. cit.,* pp. 262-267.

[25] D.C. McClelland, "Need Achievement and Entrepreneurship: A Longitudinal Study." *Journal of Personality and Social Psychology,* 1965, 1, pp. 389-392.

[26] McClelland, *The Achieving Society, op. cit.,* pp. 233-237.

[27] *Ibid.,* pp. 267-273.

[28] G.H. Litwin, "A Note on Achievement Motivation of Salesman and Sales Manager." In H. Heckhausen, *The Anatomy of Achievement Motivation.* New York: Academic Press, 1967, p. 133.

[29] B.M. Bass and G.V. Barrett, *Organization.* Boston: Allyn and Bacon, 1972, p. 61.

[30] E.G. French, "The Interaction of Achievement Motivation and Ability in Problem Solving Success." *Journal of Abnormal and Social Psychology,* 1958, 57, pp. 306-309.

[31] E.G. French and F.H. Thomas, "The Relation of Achievement Motivation to Problem Solving Effectiveness." *Journal of Abnormal and Social Psychology,* 1958, 56, pp. 46-48.

[32] A. Mehrabian, "Male and Females Tendency to Achieve." *Educational and Psychological Measurement,* 1968, 28, p. 493-502.

[33] B. Weiner and A. Kulka, "An Attributional Analysis of Achievement Motivation." *Journal of Personality and Social Psychology,* 1970, 15, pp. 1-20.

[34] K. Noujaim, "Some Motivation Determinants of Effort Allocation and Performance." (Ph.D. thesis, Sloan School of Management, MIT, 1968), cited in David A. Kolb et al., *Organizational Psychology: An Experimental Approach.* Englewood Cliffs, N.J.: Prentice-Hall, 1971, p. 71.

[35] E.G. French, "Motivation as a Variable in Work Partner Selection." *Journal of Abnormal and Social Psychology,* 1956, 53, pp. 96-99.

[36] Veroff, et al., *op. cit.,* p. 23.

[37] Meyer, Walker and Litwin, *loc. cit.*

[38] McClelland, *The Achieving Society, loc. cit.*

[39] J. Misumi and F. Seki, "Effects of Achievement Motivation on the Effectiveness of Leadership Patterns." *Administrative Science Quarterly*, 1971, 16, pp. 51-59.

[40] R. Horowitz, "nAch Correlates and The Executive Role." In G.H. Litwin and Robert A. Stringer: *Motivation and Organizational Climate.* Boston: Division of Research, Harvard Business School, 1968, p. 49.

[41] G.H. Litwin and R.A. Stringer, *Motivation and Organizational Climate.* Boston: Division of Research, Harvard Business School, 1968.

[42] *Ibid.,* p. 54.

[43] *Ibid.,* p. 75.

[44] McClelland, *The Achieving Society, loc. cit.*

[45] H. Schrage, "The R & D Entrepreneur Profile of Success." *Harvard Business Review,* November-December, 1965, pp. 56-69.

[46] H.A. Wainer and I.M. Rubin, "Motivation of Research and Development Entrepreneurs: Determinants of Company Success." *Journal of Applied Psychology*, 1969, 53, pp. 178-184.

[47] *Ibid.,* p. 183.

[48] J. Andrews, "The Achievement Motive in Two Types of Organization." *Journal of Personality and Social Psychology*, 1967, 6, pp. 163-168.

[49] P.C. Cummin, "TAT Correlates of Executive Performance." *Journal of Applied Psychology*, 1967, 51, pp. 78-81.

[50] Atkinson, *Motives in Fantasy, Action, and Society, op. cit.*, p. 77.

[51] V.J. Crandall, et al., "Motivational and Ability Determinants of Young Children's Intellectual Behavior." *Child Development*, 1962, 33, pp. 643-661.

[52] *Ibid.,* p. 657.

[53] Margaret Mead, *Male and Female.* New York: Morrow, 1949.

[54] E.E. Maccoby, "Developmental Psychology." *Annual Review of Psychology*, 1964, 15, pp. 203-250.

[55] J. Kagan and H. Moss, "Stability and Validity of Achievement Fantasy." *Journal of Abnormal and Social Psychology*, 1959, 58, pp. 357-363.

[56] M.C. Shaw and B.E. Dutton, "The Use of Parent Attitude Research Inventory with Parents of Bright Academic Underachievers." *Journal of Educational Psychology*, 1962, 53, p. 206.

[57] J.E. Teahan, "Parental Attitudes and College Success." *Journal of Educational Psychology*, 1963, 54, pp. 104-109.

[58] G.S. Lesser, "Achievement Motivation in Women." In D.C. McClelland and R.S. Steele (Eds.) *Human Motivation: A Book of Readings*. Morristown, N.J.: General Learning Press, 1973, p. 210.

[59] Rhoda Baruch, "The Achievement Motive in College Women." In D.C. McClelland and R.S. Steele (Eds.) *Human Motivation: A Book of Readings*. Morristown, N.J.: General Learning Press, 1973, p. 215.

[60] Veroff, et al., *op. cit.,* pp. 23-26.

[61] Rose E. Knotts, "Manifest Needs of Professional Female Workers in Business-Related Occupations." *Journal of Business Research,* 1975, 3, pp. 267-276.

[62] Beverlee Anderson and Ward J. McDowell, "The Corporate Woman of Tomorrow: Personality and Attitudes." Unpublished paper, University of Cincinnati, 1976.

[63] S.L. Jacobs, "Achievement Motivation and Relevant Achievement Contexts: A Revised Methodology." Unpublished Doctoral Dissertation, University of Nebraska, 1971.

[64] H. Podhoretz, "Motivation of Female Doctoral Students: Manifest Needs, Perceived Parenting and Locus of Control." Unpublished Doctoral Dissertation, Forham University, 1974.

[65] A.R. Bloom, "Achievement Motivation and Occupational Choice: A Study of Adolescent Girls." Unpublished Doctoral Dissertation, Bryn Mawr College, 1971.

[66] R.A. Frerking, "Occupational Studies of Mothers as a Determinant of Achievement Motivation in Women." Unpublished Doctoral Dissertation, University of Alabama, 1974.

[67] M.D. Vernon, *Human Motivation.* London: Cambridge University Press, 1969, p. 125.

[68] A.H. Stein and M.M. Bailey, "The Socialization of Achievement Orientation in Females." *Psychological Bulletin,* 1973, 80, p. 363.

[69] J. Veroff and T.E. Shipley, Jr., "A Projective Measure of Need for Affiliation." In J. W. Atkinson (Ed.) *Motives in Fantasy, Action, and Society,* Princeton: Van Nostrand, 1955, pp. 83-94.

[70] H.F. Harlow, "The Nature of Love." *American Psychologists,* 1958, 13, pp. 673-685.

[71] B. Berelson and G.A. Steiner, *Human Behavior.* New York: Harcourt Brace and World, Inc., 1964, p. 252.

[72] S. Schachter, *The Psychology of Affiliation.* Stanford University Press, 1959.

[73] *Ibid.*

[74] D.P. Crowne and D. Marlowe, *The Approval Motive.* New York: John Wiley and Sons, 1964, p. 202.

[75] Vernon, *op. cit.,* p. 105.

[76] E.L. Walker and R.W. Heyns, *An Anatomy of Conformity,* Englewood Cliffs, N.J.: Prentice Hall, 1962.

[77] E.P. Hollander and R.A. Willis, "Some Current Issues in the Psychology of Conformity and Non-conformity." *Psychological Bulletin,* 1967, 68, pp. 62-76.

[78] M. Jahode, "Conformity and Independence." *Human Relations,* 1959, 12, pp. 98-100.

[79] E.J. Murray, *Motivation and Emotion.* Englewood Cliffs, N.J.: Prentice Hall, 1964, pp. 101-102.

[80] French and Thomas, *loc. cit.*

[81] French, *loc. cit.*

[82] H. Rosenfield, "Social Choice Conceived as a Level of Aspiration." *Journal of Abnormal and Social Psychology,* 1964, 3, pp. 491-499.

[83] W.H. Whyte, *The Organization Man.* New York: Simon and Schuster, 1956.

[84] J.W. Atkinson, et al., "The Effect of Experimental Arousal of the Affiliation Motive on Thematic Apperception." *Journal of Abnormal and Social Psychology,* 1954, 49, pp. 405-410.

[85] H.A. Burdick and A.J. Burnes, "A Test of Strain toward Symmetry Theories." *Journal of Abnormal and Social Psychology,* 1958, 57, pp. 267-370.

[86] McClelland, *The Achieving Society, loc. cit.*

[87] Meyer, Walker and Litwin, *loc. cit.*

[88] Wainer and Rubin, *loc. cit.*

[89] Andrews, *loc. cit.*

[90] Cummins, *loc. cit.*

[91] R. DeCharms, "Affiliation Motivation and Productivity in Small Groups." *Journal of Abnormal and Social Psychology,* 1957, 55, pp. 222-226.

[92] R.E. Boyatzis, "The Need for Close Relationships and the Manager's Job." In D.A. Kolb, Irwin M. Rubin, and J.M. McIntyre (Eds.) *Organizational Psychology: A Book of Readings.* Englewood Cliffs, N.J.: Prentice-Hall, 1974, pp. 183-188.

[93] *Ibid.,* p. 184.

[94] P.R. Lawrence and J.W. Lorsch, "New Management Job: The Integrator." *Harvard Business Review,* 1967, 45, pp. 142-151.

[95] D.A. Kolb and R.E. Boyatzis, "On the Dynamics of the Helping Relationship." In D.A. Kolb, I.M. Rubin, and J.M. McIntyre (Eds.) *Organizational Psychology: A Book of Readings,* Englewood Cliffs, N.J.: Prentice-Hall, 1974, pp. 371-387.

[96] R.V. Exline, "Effects of Sex, Norms, and Affiliation Motivation upon Accuracy of Perception of Interpersonal Preference." *Journal of Personality,* 1960, 28, pp. 397-412.

[97] R.V. Exline, "Need Affiliation as Initial Communication Behavior in Problemsolving Groups Characterized by Low Interpersonal Visibility." *Psychological Report,* 1962, 10, pp. 79-89.

[98] Veroff, *loc. cit.*

[99] Warren G. Bennis, "Conversation with Warren Bennis." *Organization Dynamics,* 1974, 2, p. 62.

[100] David G. Winter, *The Power Motive.* New York: The Free Press, Collier MacMillan Publishers, 1973, p. 4.

[101] *American Heritage Dictionary.* Boston: Massachusetts, Houghton Mifflin Company, 1973.

[102] Winter, *op. cit.,* p. 5.

[103] Alfred Adler, *Social Interest.* London: Faber & Faber, Ltd., 1938.

[104] M. Weber, *The Theory of Social and Economic Organization.* Translated by T. Parsons and A.M. Henderson, London: Oxford University Press, 1947.

[105] J.R.P. French and B. Raven, "The Bases of Social Power." In D. Cartwright and A.F. Zander (Eds.) *Group Dynamics.* Evanston, Ill.: Row, Peterson, and Company, 1960, pp. 607-623.

[106] R. Christie and F.L. Geis, "Studies in Machiavellianism." In Jeanne Marecek, "Power and Women's Psychological Disorders." Paper presented at the American Psychological Association, Chicago, 1975.

[107] A. Etzioni, *A Comparative Analysis of Complex Organizations.* New York: The Free Press, 1961.

[108] Winter, *op. cit.,* pp. 17-18.

[109] *Ibid.,* p. 113.

[110] Joseph Veroff, "Development and Validation of Projective Measure of Power Motivation." *Journal of Abnormal and Social Psychology,* 1957, 54, pp. 1-9.

[111] D.C. McClelland and D.G. Winter, *Motivating Economic Achievement.* New York: The Free Press, 1969.

[112] Veroff, *loc. cit.*

[113] Litwin and Stringer, *op. cit.,* pp. 57-58.

[114] *Ibid.,* p. 74.

[115] *Ibid.,* p. 75.

[116] Winter, *op. cit.* pp. 99-101.

[117] *Ibid.,* pp. 105-106.

[118] McClelland, Need Achievement and Entrepreneurship, *loc. cit.*

[119] Veroff, et al., *loc. cit.*

[120] D.C. McClelland, "The Two Faces of Power." *Journal of International Affairs,* 1970, 24, p. 31.

[121] Cummin, *loc. cit.*

[122] Andrews, *loc. cit.*

[123] Wainer and Rubin, *loc. cit.*

[124] McClelland, *The Achieving Society, loc. cit.*

[125] D.C. McClelland and D.M. Burnham, "Power Is the Great Motivator." *Harvard Business Review,* March 1976, pp. 100-110.

[126] M. Mead, "Marriage and Family: From Popping the Question to Popping the Pill." *McCalls,* April 1976, p. 166.

[127] David G. Winter, "Power Motives and Power Behavior in Women." Paper presented at the American Psychological Association Convention, Chicago, 1975.

[128] A.J. Stewart, "Power Arousal and Thematic Apperception." Paper presented at the American Psychological Association Convention, Chicago, 1975.

[129] *Ibid.*

[130] Veroff, et al., *loc. cit.*

[131] S. Wilsnack, "The Effects of Social Drinking on Women's Fantasy." *Journal of Personality,* 1974, 42, pp. 43-61.

[132] Winter, *Power Motives and Power Behavior in Women. loc. cit.*

[133] *Ibid.*

CHAPTER III

RESEARCH METHODOLOGY

Objective

The objective of this study was to determine how strongly women managers were motivated to seek achievement, affiliation, and power, and to what extent these motives were related to their preference for male or female superiors, subordinates, and co-workers. Furthermore, an attempt was made to explore any relationships between age, occupation, personal background and their need for achievement, affiliation, and power.

Subjects

Sixty-one women managers from seven different companies in the Dayton Metropolitan Area participated in the study. Due to the comparative scarcity of women managers in any one company, an extensive search was made to locate women managers in the same geographical area. The sample size was determined by convenience sample method. The single most important element in finding an adequate sample of women managers was to receive cooperation from various employers. About a dozen companies were contacted and seven agreed to participate in this study. Considering the problem of locating women managers, the necessity of cooperation from various employers, and the amount of time required to administer the various tests, the convenience sample procedure was deemed most desirable. Although the subjects were selected by convenience, the sample consisted of managers with a wide range of background and experience. It was also agreed that the employer would not discuss the purpose of this study with the participants. This was done to elicit a normal motivational level.

Although various studies have used different sample sizes, the sample for this study was consistent with McClelland's[1] study of fifty businessmen, Cummin's[2] study of fifty-one businessmen, and Wainer and Rubin's[3] study of fifty-one entrepreneurs. A large sample size is desirable. However, for this study it was not possible to obtain more than sixty-one subjects in one geographical area without soliciting a large number of relatively small organizations.

The subjects in this study were employed in manufacturing and service type industries. Thirty-one managers worked in manufacturing, and thirty were employed in service type industries. Their job titles ranged from "supervisor" to "director."

Most of the subjects were 25 years of age and over. Table 3.1 illustrates

TABLE 3.1
AGE GROUPING OF SUBJECTS

Age	Number in Age Group	Percent in Age Group
0 to 25	5	8.2
26 to 32	21	34.4
33 to 39	9	14.8
40 to 46	10	16.4
47 to 53	9	14.8
54 and over	7	11.5
TOTAL	61	100.0

TABLE 3.2
MARITAL STATUS OF SUBJECTS

Marital Status	Number of Subjects	Percent of Subjects
Single	18	29.5
Married	37	60.7
Engaged	1	1.6
Divorced	3	4.9
Widowed	2	3.3
TOTAL	61	100.0

the age breakdown of the subjects. The subjects were mostly married, and Table 3.2 shows the marital status of the group.

Most of the subjects had some college education. Table 3.3 illustrates the educational level of the participants. Their median income was between $10,000 and $14,999. Table 3.4 presents the income level of the subjects. Their experience in managerial positions ranged from 1 to 20 years (Table A.6, in the Appendix), and most of them had received more than 2 promotions in the last five years (Table A.7, in the Appendix). Like male managers they also subscribe to *Fortune, Business Week, Newsweek,* and *Time* magazines. Overall the subjects were in their thirties and forties, well educated, well experienced, and for the most part received substantial incomes.

Instrument

The instrument used in this study was McClelland's Thematic Apperception Test (TAT) designed to measure need for achievement, affiliation, and power. There is considerable body of research to indicate that "TAT can predict organizationally relevant performance."[4] Moreover, the validity of "projective

TABLE 3.3
EDUCATIONAL LEVEL OF SUBJECTS

Education	Number of Subjects	Percent of Subjects
Some High School	1	1.6
High School Graduate	16	26.2
Some College	24	39.3
College Graduate	13	21.3
Master's & Ph.D.	7	11.5
TOTAL	61	100.0

TABLE 3.4
INCOME LEVEL OF SUBJECTS

Income	Number of Subjects	Percent of Subjects
0 to 9,999	4	6.6
10,000 to 14,999	27	44.3
15,000 to 19,999	19	31.1
20,000 to 24,999	8	13.1
25,000 and over	3	4.9
TOTAL	61	100.0

measures other than the TAT is negligible."[5] These considerations led to the selection of TAT.

The TAT (Thematic Apperception Test) was administered under neutral conditions. This was done to elicit a normal motivational level such as usually exists. Nothing is deliberately done before the administration of the test to arouse a particular kind of motivation or to relax the subject.

The set of pictures used in this study was the same as those used by Veroff, Atkinson, Feld, and Gurin[6] (1960) in a nation-wide study of 1,619 male and female adults. These pictures produced an adequate balance of scores for the three motives. The pictures selected are listed in order of presentation:

1. Two women standing by a table and one woman working with test tubes.
2. Woman (mother) seated by girl reclining in chair.
3. Group of four women—one standing, the others are seated, facing each other.
4. Woman kneeling and applying cover to a chair.
5. Two women preparing food in kitchen.
6. Women in foreground with men standing behind and to the left.

Using projective methods to measure motivation, the experimenter controls the amount of time the subjects spend writing a story. Each subject was given a booklet consisting of instruction sheets and an answer sheet (on 8½" x 14" paper). The following four questions were printed at equally spaced intervals:

1. What is happening? Who are the persons?
2. What has led up to the situation? That is, what has happened in the past?
3. What is being thought? What is wanted? By whom?
4. What will happen? What will be done?

The following instructions, as suggested by Atkinson,[7] were read to the subjects by the experimenter:

> You are going to see a series of pictures, and your task is to tell a story that is suggested to you by each picture. Try to imagine what is going on in each picture. Then tell what the situation is, what led up to the situation, what the people are thinking and feeling, and what they will do.
>
> In other words, write as complete a story as you can—a story with plot and characters.
>
> You will have 20 seconds to look at a picture and then four minutes to write your story about it. Write your first impressions and work rapidly. I will keep time and tell you when it is time to finish your story and to get ready for the next picture.
>
> There are no right or wrong stories or kinds of pictures, so you may feel free to write whatever story is suggested to you when you look at a picture. Spelling, punctuation, and grammar are not important. What is important is to write out as fully and as quickly as possible the story that comes to your mind as you imagine what is going on in each picture.
>
> Notice that there is one page for writing each story. If you need more space for writing any story, use the reverse side of the paper.

The room was darkened for twenty seconds while the first thematic picture was projected by the experimenter on a screen before the subjects. After twenty seconds the picture was turned off, the lights were turned on and the subjects began to write on the answer sheets. One minute was allowed for each question, at the end of which time the experimenter said, "It is time to go to the next question." About thirty seconds before the end of the fourth minute the experimenter said, "Try to finish up in about thirty seconds." No more than fifteen seconds (beyond the four minute limit) were allowed to finish the story. The lights were dimmed again and the next picture was projected on the screen for twenty seconds and the procedure repeated for each picture as outlined above.

Administration of Questionnaire

After completing the TAT subjects were asked to complete a questionnaire (Exhibit 1, in the Appendix). The questionnaire consisted of items related to work (type of organization in which they preferred to work, number of promotions they had received, and other demographic information such as age, income, education, etc.).

The total experiment (administration of TAT and the questionnaire) lasted for approximately forty minutes.

Coding the Data

The thematic stories for nAch and nAff were coded according to the method of content analysis described in Atkinson.[8] N-Pow scores were coded according to the method prescribed by Winter.[9] These scores provided the measure for achievement, affiliation, and power motivation. The higher the score, the more evidence of imagery in a particular motive.

In scoring for achievement motivation, one must determine whether the story contains any achievement imagery (e.g., some reference to competition with a standard of excellence or statements about a long-term achievement goal). The presence of achievement imagery is a necessary condition before other sub-categories can be scored. These sub-categories are: Need (or goal setting); Instrumental Activity; Anticipatory Goal States; Obstacles or Blocks; Affective States; Nurturant Press; and Achievement Thema. Each story written by a subject is scored by means of those categories which are appropriate to it, and the "nAch score for a particular person is the sum of the scores obtained on all of the stories written by that person. Need achievement scores on a different person are only comparable when the scores are obtained from the same pictures."[10] The maximum feasible score for one story is +11.

For the purpose of measuring, the affiliation motive has been defined "as a concern for establishing, maintaining, or restoring a positive affective relationship with another person."[11] This relationship is most adequately described by the word "friendship." A reliable measure of need for affiliation using the modified TAT procedure of McClelland has been established by Shipley and Veroff.[12]

In scoring for affiliation motive, one must determine the affiliation imagery. The presence of affiliation imagery is a prerequisite for scoring other related sub-categories. These sub-categories are: Need; Instrumental Activity; Anticipatory Goal State; Affective State; Environmental Obstacle; and Thema.[13] The maximum feasible score for one story is +7.

The power motive has been defined as "concern about establishing, maintaining, or restoring his or (her) prestige or power."[14] The method of measuring the power motivation has been subject to criticism, but numerous investigators have worked on different types of measurement systems to render the TAT more useful. Various experts have attempted to overcome such problems as reliability, scoring biases, and fallacy, in hopes of producing an instrument which merits professional acceptance. Winter has taken what, he feels, are the salient features of these systems and has re-worked them to offer the revised nPow scoring system.[15]

The method of scoring stories written in response to TAT for power motivation closely parallels the pattern established for the achievement and affiliation motives. In scoring for power motives one must consider the presence of power imagery: some reference to the thoughts, feelings, and actions of one of the characters in a story which indicates that the character is concerned with the control of the means of influencing another person. After establishing the presence of power imagery, then only can the sub-categories be scored. These sub-categories include: Prestige; Need; Instrumental Activity; Goal Anticipation; Goal States; and Effect.[16] The maximum possible score for one story is +11.

The scoring procedure to measure nAch, nAff, and nPow depends on the action or feelings depicted in the story. The scoring system has been standardized to allow self-training with the use of a manual so that a novice can quickly develop sufficient expertise in scoring stories. Each story is scored separately for each of the motives. A maximum possible score on the six story test is 66 for achievement and power, and 42 for affiliation. The test is well validated and the validations stem from various studies investigating relationships between the three motives on the one hand, and features of behavior, role, status, upbringing, and other variables on the other hand.

Methodological Consideration of TAT

The preferred scoring system in terms of usage for research purposes is that of McClelland and his associates. The system is well documented and supported by Atkinson and Winter.[17, 18]

The system of content analysis developed for each of these needs, like any other objective method of analysis, can be employed by any investigator. The protocol obtained from the subjects must be scored by judges and scorers as prescribed in the manual. Good interjudge scoring agreement has been reported, even when one judge has had relatively little experience. A review of the published research using the content analysis revealed interjudge scoring reliability in the range of .82 to .95 for nAch. Score-rescore reliability in the range of .88 to .95 has been reported. For nAff, interjudge scoring reliability of over .90 and score-rescore reliability of .89 have been reported.[19] Research utilizing nPow has yielded category agreement above .91 and rank order correlation of .84.[20]

Scoring criteria are clearly specified. Instructions and practice materials for learning the method of content analysis enable even an inexperienced coder to attain acceptable interjudge scoring reliability. Scoring reliability of the author who scored all of the protocols with expert scoring of stories was .94 for nAch, .91 for nAff, and .89 for nPow (Spearman rank order–Correlation Coefficient). Interjudge scoring reliability of the author and an independent expert scorer for a fifty percent sample of the responses (35 of 61) was .91 for nAch, .89 for nAff, and .90 for nPow. In addition a sample of one dozen protocols was scored by a professional company in the Boston area. The interjudge scoring reliability of the author and this professional company was .93 for nAch, . 91 for nAff, and .90 for nPow.[21]

In this chapter specific techniques employed in selecting subjects, instrument along with the relevant demographic information about the subjects were discussed. An analysis of data by the total population and by the industry will be reported in Chapter IV.

NOTES

[1] David E. McClelland, *The Achieving Society,* Princeton: Van Nostrand, 1961.

[2] P.C. Cummin, "TAT Correlates of Executive Performance." *Journal of Applied Psychology,* 1967, 55, pp. 78-81.

[3] H.A. Wainer and I.M. Rubin, "Motivation of Research & Development Entrepreneurs. Determinants of Company Success." *Journal of Applied Psychology,* 1969, 53, pp. 178-184.

[4] Abraham K. Korman, *Industrial and Organizational Psychology,* Englewood Cliffs, N.J.: Prentice-Hall, 1971, p. 235.

[5] Benjamin Schneider, *Staffing Organizations.* Pacific Palisades, California: Good Year Publishing, 1976. p. 178.

[6] Joseph Veroff, et al., "The Use of Thematic Apperception to Assess Motivation in a Nationwide Interview Study." *Psychological Monographs,* 1960, 94 (12, Whole No. 499).

[7] J.W. Atkinson, *Motives in Fantasy, Action, and Society.* Princeton: Van Nostrand, 1958, p. 837.

[8] Atkinson, *op. cit.,* pp. 179-218.

[9] David G. Winter, *The Power Motive.* New York: The Free Press, Collier-MacMillan Publishers, 1973.

[10] Atkinson, *loc. cit.*

[11] Roger W. Heynes, et al., "A Scoring Manual for the Affiliation Motive." In J.W. Atkinson (Ed.) *Motives in Fantasy, Action, and Society.* Princeton: Van Nostrand, 1958, pp. 179-294.

[12] J. Veroff and T. E. Shipley, Jr., "A Projective Measure of Need for Affiliation." In J.W. Atkinson (Ed.) *Motives in Fantasy, Action, and Society,* Princeton: Van Nostrand, 1958, pp. 83-94.

[13] Atkinson, *loc. cit.*

[14] Winter, *op. cit.,* p. 69.

[15] Ibid., pp. 62-95.

[16] Ibid., pp. 249-261.

[17] Atkinson, *loc. cit.*

[18] Winter, *loc. cit.*

[19] Sheila Feld and Charles Smith, "An Evaluation of the Objectivity of the Method of Content Analysis." In J.W. Atkinson (Ed.) *Motives in Fantasy, Action, and Society.* Princeton: Van Nostrand, 1958, pp. 234-235.

[20] Winter, *op. cit.*, p. 92.

[21] McBer and Company. Cambridge, Massachusetts.

CHAPTER IV

DATA ANALYSIS AND RESULTS

The results of the data analysis and the methods employed in testing the hypothesis stated in Chapter I will be discussed in this chapter.

General Statistics

Motives. The achievement motivation scores for the total sample ranged from 0 to 16 (Table A.26, in the Appendix), with a mean of 6.53 and a standard deviation (SD) of 4.11. The median was 6. For affiliation motivation the scores ranged from 0 to 15 (Table A.27, in the Appendix) with a mean of 5.45 and a standard deviation (SD) of 3.44. The median fell between 4 and 5. The power motivation scores ranged from 0 to 12 (Table A.28 in the Appendix) with a mean of 3.97 and a standard deviation (SD) of 2.84. The median fell between 3 and 4. Table 4.1 illustrates the scores.[1]

TABLE 4.1
Mean, Standard Deviation (SD), and Median for n Ach, n Aff, and n Pow of the Total Sample

Motives	Mean	SD	Median
Achievement	6.53	4.11	6.0
Affiliation	5.45	3.44	4.0
Power	3.97	2.84	3.0
N = 61			

The scores obtained for the two groups were divided into two groups: scores of managers employed in manufacturing and scores of those employed in the service sector. The achievement (nAch) scores for subjects employed in the manufacturing sector ranged from 0 to 16 with a mean of 7.58 and a standard deviation (SD) of 4.60. The median fell between 7 and 8. For nAch affiliation motivation the scores ranged from 0 to 13 with a mean of 3.52 and a standard deviation (SD) of 2.54. The median fell between 2 and 3. The power motivation scores ranged from 0 to 12 with a mean of 5.10 and a standard deviation (SD) of 2.98. The median fell between 4 and 5.

The scores of managers employed in the service sector were markedly different. The nAch scores ranged from 0 to 13 with a mean of 5.43 and a standard deviation (SD) of 3.30. The median fell between 5 and 6. The nAff scores ranged from 0 to 15 with a mean of 7.5 and a standard deviation (SD) of 3.08. The median fell between 7 and 8. For power motivation the scores ranged from 0 to 9 with a mean of 2.8 and a standard deviation (SD) of 2.1. The median fell between 2 and 3. Table 4.2 shows the scores of the two groups.

Table 4.2
Mean and Standard Deviation (SD)
for n Ach, n Aff, and n Pow by Industry Type

Industry Type	N	Mean Ach	SD	Mean Aff	SD	Mean Pow	SD
Manufacturing	31	7.58	4.60	3.52	2.54	5.10	2.98
Service	30	5.43	3.30	7.50	3.08	2.80	2.19

The subjects were then divided into three different categories: high, moderate, and low scores on need for achievement, affiliation, and power. The high motive category was established by adding one half of the computed standard deviation to the mean motive score. The low motive category was created by subtracting one half of the standard deviation from the mean motive score. Scores between the high and low were classified as moderate. These categories were established arbitrarily. Table 4.3 shows the distribution of high, moderate, and low scores for the total sample and Table 4.4 shows the distribution of scores for the two sectors (manufacturing and service).

Preference for Supervisor, Subordinate, and Co-worker. By the means of a questionnaire, the subjects were asked to indicate whether they were currently working for a male or female supervisor, the number of females and males working for them, and the number of female and male co-workers (peers) they had in the job. The questionnaire also asked for the sex of their most important subordinate and co-worker. In addition they were asked if they preferred males or females as supervisors, subordinates, and co-workers.

Eighty-five percent of the subjects worked for a male supervisor and fifteen percent had female supervisors. All subjects employed in the manufacturing sector were working for males, while seventy percent of those working in the service sector had male supervisors (Table A.8, in the Appendix).

The median number of subordinates supervised by subjects was between 3 and 4, and the median for the number of immediate co-workers fell between 2 and 3 (Tables A.9 and A.10, in the Appendix).

Fifty-six percent of the subjects rated their most important subordinate to be female. Fifty-three percent rated their most important co-worker to be

TABLE 4.3
High, Moderate, and Low Scores on
n Ach, n Aff, n Pow for the Total Sample

Motives	Number of Subjects	Percent of Subjects
ACHIEVEMENT		
High	18	29.5
Moderate	21	34.4
Low	22	36.1
TOTAL	61	100.0
AFFILIATION		
High	16	26.2
Moderate	25	41.0
Low	20	32.8
TOTAL	61	100.0
POWER		
High	16	26.2
Moderate	26	42.6
Low	19	31.1
TOTAL	61	100.0

male. The analysis of data by industrial sector revealed that subjects employed in the service sector chose females as their most important subordinate (74 percent), while the subjects employed in manufacturing chose males (55 percent). Both groups selected males as their most important co-worker (service sector 54 percent; manufacturing sector 71 percent). Tables A.11 and A.12 in the Appendix show these responses.

Eighty percent of the entire sample preferred male supervisors. Respondents were about evenly divided in their preferences for male and female subordinates and co-workers. Some noticeable differences were observed between the service and the manufacturing sector. Ninety percent of the subjects employed in manufacturing preferred male supervisors, whereas seventy percent of the subjects from the service sector preferred male supervisors. While sixty-eight percent of the subjects from the manufacturing preferred male subordinates, only thirty percent of women managers in the service sector preferred male subordinates. There was no significant difference in their sex preferences for co-workers (Tables A.13, A.14, and A.15, in the Appendix).

Organizational Preference. As expected the analysis of data by industry revealed that subjects employed in the manufacturing sector generally preferred to work for a manufacturing sector and the subjects employed in the service sector preferred to work in a service sector. The most important reason

DATA ANALYSIS AND RESULTS

TABLE 4.4
MOTIVE SCORES FOR THE TWO GROUPS

Motives	Managers Employed in Manufacturing Sector (N =31)		Managers Employed in Service Sector (N = 30)	
	Number of Subjects	Percent of Subjects	Number of Subjects	Percent of Subjects
ACHIEVEMENT				
High	13	41.9	5	16.7
Moderate	5	16.1	18	60.0
Low	13	42.0	7	23.3
TOTAL	31	100.0	30	100.0
AFFILIATION				
High	8	25.8	10	33.3
Moderate	10	32.3	9	30.0
Low	13	41.9	11	36.7
TOTAL	31	100.0	30	100.0
POWER				
High	10	32.3	10	33.3
Moderate	13	41.9	11	36.7
Low	8	25.9	9	30.0
TOTAL	31	100.0	30	100.0

for their preference for a particular type of organization was "challenge" (sixty-two percent). Fifteen percent indicated "growth," and seven percent rated "salary" as the most important reason. The data for the two groups revealed no significant difference (Table A.16, in the Appendix).

Analysis of Hypotheses. Hypotheses 1 stated that women managers are not significantly different from women in general in their need for achievement, affiliation, and power. These comparisons were based on the data obtained by Veroff and his associates in a nation-wide study of 774 women in general.[2] A Z test was employed to compare differences between the mean motive scores of women managers and women in general.[3] The resulting data showed some significant differences. Consequently the null Hypothesis 1 was rejected. The Z value obtained for the achievement motive was 9.57 which is significant ($p < .0001$). The Z value for the power motive was 5.98 which is significant ($p < .001$). The Z value obtained for the affiliation motive was .567, indicating there is no significant difference in the level of affiliation motivation of women managers and women in general. The results suggest that women managers have a higher need for achievement and power than women in general. Table 4.5 presents comparative data on three motives.

DATA ANALYSIS AND RESULTS 49

TABLE 4.5
Comparison of Motive Scores of Women
Managers with Women in General

Women Managers Motive	(N = 61) Mean	SD	Women in General (N = 774) Mean	SD	Z value	p
Achievement	6.53	4.11	3.97	3.30	9.57	.0001
Affiliation	5.45	3.44	5.31	3.54	.567	.5
Power	3.97	2.84	1.84	2.19	9.58	.0001

Hypothesis 2 stated that women managers do not differ significantly in their need for achievement, affiliation, and power, irrespective of the type of industry in which they are employed: manufacturing or service sector. A student's t-test was used to compare the differences between the mean achievement, affiliation, and power scores of the two groups.[4] The results showed some significant differences between the two groups. Accordingly, the null Hypothesis 2 was also rejected. Table 4.6 shows the comparison between the means for the achievement, affiliation, and power motives of the two groups.

TABLE 4.6
Comparison of Motive Scores of Women Managers
Employed in Manufacturing and Service Sectors

Motive	N	Mean	SD	T value	Significance Level
ACHIEVEMENT					
Manufacturing	31	7.58	4.56	2.10	.02
Service	30	5.43	3.33		
AFFILIATION					
Manufacturing	31	3.52	2.54	-5.52	.0001
Service	30	7.50	3.08		
POWER					
Manufacturing	31	5.10	2.98	3.42	.0005
Service	30	2.80	2.19		

The t value obtained for nAch was 2.10, which is significant (p < .02). For affiliation motive, the t value was -5.52, which is significant (p < .0001). The t value for nPow was 3.42, which is significant (p < .0005). The results indicate that women managers employed in the manufacturing sector are significantly different from women managers employed in the service sector in their need for achievement, affiliation, and power. Apparently, women managers employed in manufacturing have a greater need for achievement and power and a lower need for affiliation than their service sector counterparts.

Hypothesis 3 stated that there are no significant relationships between the motives and the women managers' preferences for male-female supervisors, subordinates, and co-workers. The subjects were divided into three motivational categories: high, moderate, and low for each of the three needs: nAch, nAff, and nPow. As noted previously, these categories were established by adding and subtracting one half of the computed standard deviations to the mean motive scores. A chi-square test was applied to determine the existence of any significant relationship between the motives and their preference for a male or female supervisor, subordinate, and co-worker.

The results obtained for the total sample do not indicate a relationship between motives and preference for supervisor's sex. The chi-square value obtained for the achievement, affiliation, and power motives were 3.82, 2.54, and .734 respectively, indicating no significant relationships. Table 4.7 outlines the results.

The results for the total sample indicate significant relationships between motives and preference for subordinate sex. The chi-square value obtained for achievement motive was 6.06 (p < .05). The chi-square value for affiliation motive was 8.48 (p < .01), indicating a relationship exists between motives and preference for subordinate's sex. Supporting results are presented in Table 4.8.

The analysis of results presented for the total sample does not support any strong relationship between motives and preference for co-worker's sex. The results are presented in Table 4.9.

Based on the results, Hypothesis 3 was partially confirmed. The results imply that women managers generally prefer male supervisors. Possibly, they have a slight preference for female co-workers. However, women managers with a high need for achievement and power and a low need for affiliation prefer male subordinates. Women managers with a moderate or low need for achievement, a high or moderate need for affiliation, and a moderate or a low need for power prefer female subordinates. Preference for male subordinates appears to be related to a high need for achievement and power and preference for female subordinates seems to be related to a high or moderate need for affiliation and a low need for achievement and power.

The analysis of data by industrial sector did indicate some relationships. For women managers employed in manufacturing, there were significant relationships between achievement motive and preference for supervisor's sex. The chi-square value was 6.71, which is significant (p < .03). The chi-square value for both the affiliation and power motive was not significant. The results are stated in Table 4.10. The results stated in Table 4.11 do not support any relationships between motives and preferences for subordinate or co-worker's sex.

For women managers employed in either industrial sector, there was no relationship between the three motives and preferences for supervisor, subordinate, and co-worker's sex. However, the results suggest that respondents tend to prefer male supervisors, female subordinates, and female co-workers. Tables

4.12, 4.13, 4.14, and 4.15 support this conclusion.

The overall results indicate that women managers from both sectors prefer male supervisors. Women managers employed in manufacturing prefer male subordinates while women managers employed in the service sector tend to prefer female subordinates and co-workers.

Relationship Between the Three Needs. The correlation between the motives shown in Table 4.16 indicates that the motives are related to each other. The achievement motive is positively related to power motive and the power motive is negatively related to affiliation motive. The results imply that managers with a high need for achievement also have a high need for power and managers with a high need for power have a low need for affiliation. The relationship between the achievement motive and the affiliation motive is not significant.

Relationship Between Motives and Other Variables

Relationship Between Motives and Organizational Preference. As noted above, the analysis of data for the total sample indicated that women managers prefer to work for the sector in which they are employed. Although "challenge" was the most important reason for their preference, the results did not indicate any significant relationships between motives and their reasons for organizational preference. The chi-square value for the motives and organizational preference was not significant. Other information obtained was the fact that the managers rated salary, stability, and social responsibility as the least important reasons for organizational preference (Tables 4.17, 4.18, and 4.19).

The results for the two industrial sectors showed some significant relationships. For managers employed in manufacturing, the level of achievement motive was related to their reasons for organizational preference. The chi-square value of 14.78 for achievement is significant ($p < .06$). The chi-square values for affiliation and power motives were not significant. The results stated in Tables 4.18 and 4.19 indicate that for both industrial sectors, challenge is by far the most important reason for organizational preference. This finding is quite independent of motive strength.

Relationship Between Motives and Job Position in the Company. The achievement and power motives for the total sample appear to be unrelated to the position held by the subjects. The chi-square values obtained for job positions and achievement and power do not indicate a strong relationship. However, the level of affiliation motive was found to be related to position. The chi-square value of 11.59 is significant ($p < .07$). The results in Table 4.20 showed that subjects with a high need for affiliation occupied upper level positions in the hierarchy (managers) and subjects with a moderate or low need for affiliation occupied lower level positions (supervisors). The results obtained for the women managers employed in manufacturing and the service sector did not show any relationship between job position and the three motives.

Relationship Between Education and Motives. Although most of the subjects had some college education, the results for the total sample do not show any relationship between education and the three motives (Table 4.21). For women managers employed in manufacturing, the achievement motive was related to education. The chi-square value of 15.55 is significant ($p < .05$). Results presented in Table 4.22 indicate that managers high in achievement motivation were more educated (college graduates) than managers low in achievement motivation. Affiliation and power motivation were unrelated to education. For managers employed in the service sector the affiliation motive appears to be related to education (Table 4.23).

Furthermore, the subjects were grouped into two categories: high and low scores on the motives, and college and no college in terms of education. Scores above the median were categorized as high and scores below the median were categorized as low. Table 4.24 represents the educational level of subjects who scored high in any one of the three motives. The results indicate that the percentage of subjects (total sample and the subjects employed in manufacturing) scoring above the median in any one of the three motives with college education is higher than the percentage of high scorers with high school education. However, in the service sector, the percentage of subjects scoring above the median in any one of the three motives with high school education was substantially higher than the percentage of high scorers with college education. These results imply that the subjects from the two industrial sectors have different educational backgrounds.

Relationship Between Age and Motives. The results obtained for the total sample did not show any relationship between age and the three motives. The results for women managers employed in manufacturing, although not significant, indicated that younger women (under 40) tend to have a higher need for achievement, and older women (over 40) tend to have a lower need for achievement. For managers employed in the service sector, the results indicate that younger managers tend to be more affiliation oriented. These results are reported in Tables 4.25, 4.26, and 4.27.

Table 4.28 illustrates the age of subjects who scored above the median in each of the three motives. The data for the total sample indicate that the achievement and affiliation motives were high in the younger women managers and the power motive appears to be high among older managers. For managers employed in the manufacturing sector, the data on need for achievement and need for affiliation were similar to the total sample; however, the power motive seems to be relatively high among younger managers. In the service sector, the achievement and power motives were higher among older managers, and a higher affiliation motive was found among younger managers.

Relationship Between Income and Motives. There did not appear to be a significant relationship between income and the three motives for the total sample (Table 4.29). The results on the affiliation motive for women managers employed in manufacturing were significantly related to income. The chi-square value of 6.80 is significant (p < .03). This indicates that subjects high in need for affiliation were earning significantly more income than subjects low in affiliation. These results are reported in Table 4.30. Both affiliation and power motives were found to be related to income for subjects employed in the service sector. The chi-square value for nAff was 5.05, which is significant (p < .08). The chi-square value of 5.41 for power is also significant (p < .06). The results show that subjects with high need for power were earning significantly more than subjects with a moderate and low need for power. Also subjects with a moderate need for affiliation were earning significantly more than subjects with a low need for affiliation. These results are reported in Table 4.31.

Table 4.32 represents the income level of subjects who scored high (above the median) in any one of the three motives. The overall results indicate that the percentage of subjects scoring above the median with high income ($15,000 and over) is higher for any one of the three motives than the percentage of high scores with low income (less than $15,000).

Relationship Between Marital Status and Motives. The marital status of subjects (married or other) who scored high (above the median) in any one of the three motives is reported in Table 4.33. The results for the total sample indicate that the percentage of married subjects scoring high in affiliation and power motive is substantially higher than the percentage of subjects who were not married. However, the achievement motivation scores were found to be higher among unmarried subjects. For subjects employed in the manufacturing sector, the need for achievement, affiliation, and power scores were found to be relatively high among those who were married. In the service sector, the need for achievement and need for affiliation scores were found to be high among managers who were not married, while a high power motive was found among those who were married.

Relationship Between Years in Managerial Service and Motives. Motives were found to be unrelated to years in managerial service irrespective of industry type. The only exception was the relationship between the power motive and years in managerial service for the total sample. The chi-square value of 4.88 is significant (p < .08). Subjects high in power had significantly more years of managerial experience than subjects with moderate or low need for power. These results are illustrated in Tables 4.34, 4.35, and 4.36.

Relationship Between Consumption of Alcohol and Motives. It was found that affiliation motive for women managers employed in the service sector was related to consumption of alcohol. The chi-square value of 5.19 is significant ($p < .07$). The consumption of alcohol for subjects with a high and moderate need for affiliation was significantly higher than subjects with a low need for affiliation. There was some indication that subjects with a moderate and low need in achievement and power consumed more alcohol. However, these results were not significant. Results are stated in Table A.29, in the Appendix.

Relationship Between Smoking and Motives. For the total sample smoking was found to be related to the power motive. The chi-square value of 4.93 is significant ($p < .08$). The results imply that people with a high or low need for power are less likely to smoke than others. For subjects employed in the manufacturing sector, the achievement and power motive was found to be related to smoking. The chi-square value of 7.48 for achievement is significant ($p < .02$), and the chi-square value of 4.77 for power is also significant ($p < .09$). This indicates that subjects with high need for achievement and power are less likely to smoke than others. These results are reported in Tables A.30 and A.31 in the Appendix. Among those who smoked, subjects with a low need for achievement smoked more than subjects with a high need for achievement (Table A.32, in the Appendix).

Summary of Results

The overall results of this study stated in this chapter are summarized below.

1. Women managers tend to have a higher need for achievement and power than women in general. However, their need for affiliation is not significantly different from women in general.

2. Women managers employed in the manufacturing sector have a relatively higher need for achievement and power and a relatively lower need for affiliation.

3. Women managers employed in the service sector have a relatively higher need for affiliation, moderate need for achievement, and a relatively lower need for power.

4. Women managers tend to prefer male supervisors and female co-workers.

5. Women managers with a high need for achievement and power tend to prefer male subordinates. Managers with a high need for affiliation prefer female subordinates.

6. Women managers appear to like challenge in their job.

7. High achievers tend to have higher levels of education.

8. Younger women managers tend to have a higher need for achievement than do older women.

9. Women managers with more years of managerial experience tend to have a higher need for power than do women with fewer years of managerial experience.

10. Women managers with a high need for affiliation tend to earn higher incomes.

11. Women managers with higher need for affiliation tend to consume more alcohol, and managers with a higher need for achievement and power tend not to smoke.

A detailed analysis of data combined with the results were stated in this chapter. Chapter V will discuss the results, limitations, implications, and suggestions for future research.

TABLE 4.7
RELATIONSHIP BETWEEN MOTIVE CATEGORY AND PREFERENCE FOR SUPERVISOR'S SEX
(For the Total Sample, N = 61)

Motive Category	N	Preference for Female Supervisor	Preference for Male Supervisor	Chi-square	Significance Level
ACHIEVEMENT					
High	18	2	16		
Moderate	21	7	14	3.82	N.S.
Low	22	3	19		
AFFILIATION					
High	16	5	11		
Moderate	25	5	20	2.54	N.S.
Low	20	2	18		
POWER					
High	16	2	14		
Moderate	26	6	20	.734	N.S.
Low	19	4	15		

N.S. = Not significant at .10 level

TABLE 4.8
RELATIONSHIP BETWEEN MOTIVE CATEGORY AND PREFERENCE FOR SUBORDINATE'S SEX
(For the Total Sample, N = 61)

Motive Category	N	Preference for Female Subordinate	Preference for Male Subordinate	Chi-square	Significance Level
ACHIEVEMENT					
High	18	5	13		
Moderate	21	14	7	6.06	.05
Low	22	12	10		
AFFILIATION					
High	16	9	7		
Moderate	25	17	8	8.48	.01
Low	20	5	15		
POWER					
High	16	6	10		
Moderate	26	15	11	1.65	N.S.
Low	19	10	9		

N.S. = Not significant at .10 level

TABLE 4.9
RELATIONSHIP BETWEEN MOTIVE CATEGORY AND PREFERENCE FOR CO-WORKER'S SEX
(For the Total Sample, N = 58)*

Motive Category	N	Preference for Female Co-worker	Preference for Male Co-worker	Chi-square	Significance Level
ACHIEVEMENT					
High	17*	9	8		
Moderate	20	12	8	.18	N.S.
Low	21	12	9		
AFFILIATION					
High	16*	8	8		
Moderate	23	15	8	1.10	N.S.
Low	19	10	9		
POWER					
High	14*	8	6		
Moderate	25	16	9	1.21	N.S.
Low	19	9	10		

* indicates that 3 individuals did not have any co-workers
N.S. = not significant at .10 level

TABLE 4.10
RELATIONSHIP BETWEEN MOTIVE CATEGORY AND PREFERENCE FOR SUPERVISOR'S SEX
(For the Manufacturing Sector, N = 31)

Motive Category	N	Preference for Female Supervisor	Preference for Male Supervisor	Chi-square	Significance Level
ACHIEVEMENT					
High	13	0	13		
Moderate	5	2	3	6.71	.03
Low	13	1	12		
AFFILIATION					
High	8	0	8		
Moderate	10	1	9	1.34	N.S.
Low	13	2	11		
POWER					
High	10	1	9		
Moderate	13	2	11	1.34	N.S.
Low	8	0	8		

N.S. = not significant at .10 level

TABLE 4.11
RELATIONSHIP BETWEEN MOTIVE CATEGORY AND PREFERENCE FOR SUBORDINATE'S SEX
(For the Manufacturing Sector, N = 31)

Motive Category	N	Preference for Female Subordinate	Preference for Male Subordinate	Chi-square	Significance Level
ACHIEVEMENT					
High	13	3	10		
Moderate	5	2	3	.86	N.S.
Low	13	5	8		
AFFILIATION					
High	8	1	7		
Moderate	10	5	5	2.88	N.S.
Low	15	4	9		
POWER					
High	10	3	7		
Moderate	13	5	8	.44	N.S.
Low	8	2	6		

N.S. = not significant at .10 level

TABLE 4.12
RELATIONSHIP BETWEEN MOTIVE CATEGORY AND PREFERENCE FOR CO-WORKER'S SEX
(For the Manufacturing Sector, N = 28)*

Motive Category	N	Preference for Female Co-worker	Preference for Male Co-worker	Chi-square	Significance Level
ACHIEVEMENT					
High	12*	7	5		
Moderate	4	2	2	.19	N.S.
Low	12	6	6		
AFFILIATION					
High	7*	3	4		
Moderate	9	5	4	.44	N.S.
Low	12	7	5		
POWER					
High	8*	4	4		
Moderate	13	9	4	3.08	N.S.
Low	7	2	5		

* indicates that 3 individuals did not have any co-workers
N.S. = not significant at .10 level

TABLE 4.13
RELATIONSHIP BETWEEN MOTIVE CATEGORY AND PREFERENCE FOR SUPERVISOR'S SEX
(For the Service Sector, N = 30)

Motive Category	N	Preference for Female Supervisor	Preference for Male Supervisor	Chi-square	Significance Level
ACHIEVEMENT					
High	5	2	3		
Moderate	18	6	12	1.15	N.S.
Low	7	1	6		
AFFILIATION					
High	10	4	6		
Moderate	9	1	8	2.21	N.S.
Low	11	4	7		
POWER					
High	10	3	7		
Moderate	11	3	8	.09	N.S.
Low	9	3	6		

N.S. = not significant at .10 level

TABLE 4.14
RELATIONSHIP BETWEEN MOTIVE CATEGORY AND PREFERENCE FOR SUBORDINATE'S SEX
(For the Service Sector, N = 30)

Motive Category	N	Preference for Female Subordinate	Preference for Male Subordinate	Chi-square	Significance Level
ACHIEVEMENT					
High	5	2	3		
Moderate	18	13	5	3.01	N.S.
Low	7	6	1		
AFFILIATION					
High	10	7	3		
Moderate	9	6	3	.09	N.S.
Low	11	8	3		
POWER					
High	10	6	4		
Moderate	11	8	3	.77	N.S.
Low	9	7	2		

N.S. = not significant at .10 level

TABLE 4.15
RELATIONSHIP BETWEEN MOTIVE CATEGORY AND PREFERENCE FOR CO-WORKER'S SEX
(For the Service Sector, N = 30)

Motive Category	N	Preference for Female Co-worker	Preference for Male Co-worker	Chi-square	Significance Level
ACHIEVEMENT					
High	5	2	3		
Moderate	18	12	6	1.19	N.S.
Low	7	4	3		
AFFILIATION					
High	10	5	5		
Moderate	9	7	2	1.74	N.S.
Low	11	6	5		
POWER					
High	10	6	4		
Moderate	11	7	4	.13	N.S.
Low	9	5	4		

N.S. = not significant at .10 level

TABLE 4.16
Relationship Between the Three Needs[a]

Motive	Affiliation	Power
Achievement	-.1250	.3104**
Power	-.3573*	

[a] Pearson Correlation Coefficient Test
* (p < .005)
** (p < .015)

TABLE 4.17
RELATIONSHIP BETWEEN MOTIVE CATEGORY
AND REASONS FOR ORGANIZATIONAL PREFERENCE
(For the Total Sample, N = 61)

Motive Category	N	Reasons					Chi-square	Significance Level
		Stability	Challenge	Salary	Growth	Social Reponsibility		
ACHIEVEMENT								
High	18	2	10	0	5	1		
Moderate	21	2	14	2	2	1	4.99	N.S.
Low	22	3	14	2	2	1		
AFFILIATION								
High	16	1	11	0	3	1		
Moderate	25	3	15	3	4	0	5.84	N.S.
Low	20	3	12	1	2	2		
POWER								
High	16	1	10	1	3	1		
Moderate	26	3	18	2	2	1	2.96	N.S.
Low	19	3	10	1	4	1		

N.S. = not significant at .10 level

TABLE 4.18
RELATIONSHIP BETWEEN MOTIVE CATEGORY
AND REASONS FOR ORGANIZATIONAL PREFERENCE
(For the Manufacturing Sector, N = 31)

Motive Category	N	Reasons					Chi-square	Significance Level
		Stability	Challenge	Salary	Growth	Social Responsibility		
ACHIEVEMENT								
High	13	0	9	0	4	0		
Moderate	5	0	1	1	2	1	14.78	.06
Low	13	3	8	1	0	1		
AFFILIATION								
High	8	0	4	1	3	0		
Moderate	10	1	8	0	1	0	8.27	N.S.
Low	13	2	6	1	2	2		
POWER								
High	10	0	6	1	3	0		
Moderate	13	2	8	1	1	1	5.09	N.S.
Low	8	1	4	0	2	1		

N.S. = not significant at .10 level

TABLE 4.19
RELATIONSHIP BETWEEN MOTIVE CATEGORY
AND REASONS FOR ORGANIZATIONAL PREFERENCE
(For the Service Sector, N = 30)

Motive Category	N	Stability	Challenge	Salary	Growth	Social Responsibility	Chi-square	Significance Level
				Reasons				
ACHIEVEMENT								
High	5	2	1	0	1	1		
Moderate	18	1	14	1	2	0	12.68	N.S.
Low	7	1	5	1	0	0		
AFFILIATION								
High	10	1	7	0	1	1		
Moderate	9	0	8	0	1	0	9.78	N.S.
Low	11	3	5	2	1	0		
POWER								
High	10	1	6	1	1	1		
Moderate	11	1	10	0	0	0	8.08	N.S.
Low	9	2	4	1	2	0		

N.S. = not significant at .10 level

TABLE 4.20
RELATIONSHIP BETWEEN MOTIVE CATEGORY AND POSITION IN THE COMPANY
(For the Total Sample, N = 61)

Motive Category	N	Directors	Managers	Supervisors	Professional	Chi-square	Significance Level
ACHIEVEMENT							
High	18	1	6	9	2		
Moderate	21	0	10	11	0	7.61	N.S.
Low	22	2	7	13	0		
AFFILIATION							
High	16	0	9	7	0		
Moderate	25	3	9	13	0	11.53	.07
Low	20	0	5	13	2		
POWER							
High	16	1	7	6	2		
Moderate	26	1	11	14	0	8.23	N.S.
Low	19	1	5	13	0		

N.S. = not significant at .10 level

TABLE 4.21
RELATIONSHIP BETWEEN MOTIVE CATEGORY AND EDUCATION
(For the Total Sample, N = 61)

Motive Category	N	Some High School	High School Graduate	Some College	College Graduate	Master's or Ph.D.	Chi-square	Significance Level
ACHIEVEMENT								
High	18	0	3	6	5	4		
Moderate	21	0	8	9	4	0	8.69	N.S.
Low	22	1	5	9	4	3		
AFFILIATION								
High	16	0	3	8	3	2		
Moderate	25	0	7	8	7	3	4.34	N.S.
Low	20	1	6	8	3	2		
POWER								
High	16	0	5	7	2	2		
Moderate	26	1	7	9	6	3	2.84	N.S.
Low	19	0	4	8	5	2		

N.S. = not significant at .10 level

TABLE 4.22
RELATIONSHIP BETWEEN MOTIVE CATEGORY AND EDUCATION
(For the Manufacturing Sector, N = 31)

Motive Category	N	Some High School	High School Graduate	Some College	College Graduate	Master's or Ph.D.	Chi-square	Significance Level
ACHIEVEMENT								
High	13	0	3	2	5	3		
Moderate	5	0	1	4	0	0	15.55	.05
Low	13	1	6	4	0	2		
AFFILIATION								
High	8	0	2	1	2	3		
Moderate	10	0	4	3	2	1	7.60	N.S.
Low	13	1	4	6	1	1		
POWER								
High	10	0	3	4	1	2		
Moderate	13	1	4	3	3	2	2.92	N.S.
Low	8	0	3	3	1	1		

N.S. = not significant at .10 level

TABLE 4.23
RELATIONSHIP BETWEEN MOTIVE CATEGORY AND EDUCATION
(For the Service Sector, N = 30)

Motive Category	N	Some High School	High School Graduate	Some College	College Graduate	Master's or Ph.D.	Chi-square	Significance Level
ACHIEVEMENT								
High	5	0	0	4	0	1		
Moderate	18	0	5	7	5	1	6.97	N.S.
Low	7	0	1	3	3	0		
AFFILIATION								
High	10	0	2	7	1	0		
Moderate	9	0	2	0	5	2	14.91	.02
Low	11	0	2	7	2	0		
POWER								
High	10	0	1	6	2	1		
Moderate	11	0	5	4	2	0	9.20	N.S.
Low	9	0	0	4	4	1		

N.S. = not significant at .10 level

TABLE 4.24
RELATIONSHIP BETWEEN EDUCATION AND MOTIVES
(High Scores)[a]

Motive and Education	Total Sample		Subjects Employed in Manufacturing Sector		Subjects Employed in Service Sector	
	Number of Subjects	Percentage of Subjects	Number of Subjects	Percentage of Subjects	Number of Subjects	Percentage of Subjects
ACHIEVEMENT						
High School	8	47	3	27	4	66
College	26	59	13	65	12	50
AFFILIATION						
High School	7	41	6	54	3	50
College	25	57	12	60	11	46
POWER						
High School	9	52	5	45	4	67
College	24	54	11	55	13	54

a Subjects scoring above the median in any one of the three motives.

High school:	N = 17	11	6
College:	N = 44	20	24

TABLE 4.25
RELATIONSHIP BETWEEN MOTIVE CATEGORY AND AGE
(For the Total Sample, N = 61)

Motive Category	N	Age		Chi-square	Significance Level
		Under 40	Over 40		
ACHIEVEMENT					
High	18	12	6		
Moderate	21	9	12	2.80	N.S.
Low	22	14	8		
AFFILIATION					
High	16	11	5		
Moderate	25	15	10	2.17	N.S.
Low	20	9	11		
POWER					
High	16	9	7		
Moderate	26	13	13	1.53	N.S.
Low	19	13	6		

N.S. = not significant at .10 level

TABLE 4.26
RELATIONSHIP BETWEEN MOTIVE CATEGORY AND AGE
(For the Manufacturing Sector, N = 31)

Motive Category	N	Age		Chi-square	Significance Level
		Under 40	Over 40		
ACHIEVEMENT					
High	13	9	4		
Moderate	5	2	3	4.02	N.S.
Low	13	4	9		
AFFILIATION					
High	8	4	4		
Moderate	10	6	4	1.06	N.S.
Low	13	5	8		
POWER					
High	10	6	4		
Moderate	13	5	8	1.06	N.S.
Low	8	4	4		

N.S. = not significant at .10 level

TABLE 4.27
RELATIONSHIP BETWEEN MOTIVE CATEGORY AND AGE
(For the Service Sector, N = 30)

Motive Category	N	Age		Chi-square	Significance Level
		Under 40	Over 40		
ACHIEVEMENT					
High	5	3	2		
Moderate	18	11	7	1.49	N.S.
Low	7	6	1		
AFFILIATION					
High	10	7	3		
Moderate	9	7	2	1.27	N.S.
Low	11	6	5		
POWER					
High	10	6	4		
Moderate	11	5	6	6.93	.03
Low	9	9	0		

N.S. = not significant at .10 level

TABLE 4.28
RELATIONSHIP BETWEEN AGE AND MOTIVES
(High Scorers[a])

Motive and Education	Total Sample		Subjects Employed in Manufacturing Sector		Subjects Employed in Service Sector	
	Number of Subjects	Percentage of Subjects	Number of Subjects	Percentage of Subjects	Number of Subjects	Percentage of Subjects
ACHIEVEMENT						
under 40	20	57	9	60	9	45
over 40	14	54	7	44	7	70
AFFILIATION						
under 40	22	63	10	67	10	50
over 40	10	38	8	50	4	40
POWER						
under 40	17	49	8	53	10	50
over 40	16	61	8	50	7	70

[a] Subjects scoring above the median in any one of the three motives

under 40:	N = 35		15		20	
over 40:	N = 26		16		10	

TABLE 4.29
RELATIONSHIP BETWEEN MOTIVE CATEGORY AND INCOME
(For the Total Sample, N = 61)

Motive Category	N	Income Under $15,000	Over $15,000	Chi-square	Significance Level
ACHIEVEMENT					
High	18	8	10		
Moderate	21	12	9	.63	N.S.
Low	22	11	11		
AFFILIATION					
High	16	6	10		
Moderate	25	12	13	2.82	N.S.
Low	20	13	7		
POWER					
High	16	7	9		
Moderate	26	13	13	.71	N.S.
Low	19	11	8		

N.S. = not significant at .10 level

TABLE 4.30
RELATIONSHIP BETWEEN MOTIVE CATEGORY AND INCOME
(For the Manufacturing Sector, N = 31)

Motive Category	N	Income Under $15,000	Over $15,000	Chi-square	Significance Level
ACHIEVEMENT					
High	13	6	7		
Moderate	5	3	2	.32	N.S.
Low	13	7	6		
AFFILIATION					
High	8	1	7		
Moderate	10	6	4	6.80	.03
Low	13	9	4		
POWER					
High	10	5	5		
Moderate	13	7	6	.04	N.S.
Low	8	4	4		

N.S. = not significant at .10 level

TABLE 4.31
RELATIONSHIP BETWEEN MOTIVE CATEGORY AND INCOME
(For the Service Sector, N = 30)

Motive Category	N	Income Under $15,000	Over $15,000	Chi-square	Significance Level
ACHIEVEMENT					
High	5	2	3		
Moderate	18	9	9	.34	N.S.
Low	7	4	3		
AFFILIATION					
High	10	5	5		
Moderate	9	2	7	5.05	.08
Low	11	8	3		
POWER					
High	10	2	8		
Moderate	11	7	4	5.41	.06
Low	9	6	3		

N.S. = not significant at .10 level

TABLE 4.32
RELATIONSHIP BETWEEN INCOME AND MOTIVES
(High Scorers[a])

Motive and Income	Total Sample		Subjects Employed in Manufacturing Sector		Subjects Employed in Service Sector	
	Number of Subjects	Percentage of Subjects	Number of Subjects	Percentage of Subjects	Number of Subjects	Percentage of Subjects
ACHIEVEMENT						
0 - 14,999	17	55	7	44	8	53
15,000 and over	17	57	9	60	8	53
AFFILIATION						
0 - 14,999	12	39	7	44	6	40
15,000 and over	20	67	11	73	8	53
POWER						
0 - 14,999	14	45	8	50	7	47
15,000 and over	19	63	8	53	10	67

[a] Subjects scoring above the median in any one of the three motives

0 - 14,999	N = 31		16		15	
15,000 and over	N = 30		15		15	

TABLE 4.33
RELATIONSHIP BETWEEN MARITAL STATUS AND MOTIVES
(High Scorers[a])

Motive and Marital Status	Total Sample		Subjects Employed in Manufacturing Sector		Subjects Employed in Service Sector	
	Number of Subjects	Percentage of Subjects	Number of Subjects	Percentage of Subjects	Number of Subjects	Percentage of Subjects
ACHIEVEMENT						
Other*	14	58	6	50	8	67
Married	20	54	10	53	8	44
AFFILIATION						
Other*	11	46	6	50	6	50
Married	21	57	12	63	8	44
POWER						
Other*	12	50	6	50	6	50
Married	21	57	10	53	11	61

[a] Subjects scoring above the median in any one of the three motives

Other	N = 26	12	12
Married	N = 37	19	18

* Indicates single, divorced, widowed

TABLE 4.34
RELATIONSHIP BETWEEN MOTIVE CATEGORY
AND YEARS IN MANAGERIAL POSITION
(For the Total Sample, N = 61)

Motive Category	N	Years in Management Position		Chi-square	Significance Level
		1 to 3 years	4 or more		
ACHIEVEMENT					
High	18	10	8		
Moderate	21	13	8	.29	N.S.
Low	22	14	8		
AFFILIATION					
High	16	10	6		
Moderate	25	17	8	1.54	N.S.
Low	20	10	10		
POWER					
High	16	6	10		
Moderate	26	18	8	4.88	.08
Low	19	13	6		

N.S. = not significant at .10 level

TABLE 4.35
RELATIONSHIP BETWEEN MOTIVE CATEGORY
AND YEARS IN MANAGERIAL POSITION
(For the Manufacturing Sector, N = 31)

Motive Category	N	Years in Management Position		Chi-square	Significance Level
		1 to 3 years	4 or more		
ACHIEVEMENT					
High	13	9	4		
Moderate	5	2	3	2.27	N.S.
Low	13	10	3		
AFFILIATION					
High	8	7	1		
Moderate	10	6	4	1.93	N.S.
Low	13	8	5		
POWER					
High	10	5	5		
Moderate	13	9	4	2.88	N.S.
Low	8	7	1		

N.S. = not significant at .10 level

TABLE 4.36
RELATIONSHIP BETWEEN MOTIVE CATEGORY
AND YEARS IN MANAGERIAL POSITION
(For the Service Sector, N = 30)

Motive Category	N	Years in Management Position		Chi-square	Significance Level
		1 to 3 years	4 or more		
ACHIEVEMENT					
High	5	1	4		
Moderate	18	11	7	2.71	N.S.
Low	7	4	3		
AFFILIATION					
High	10	5	5		
Moderate	9	5	4	.07	N.S.
Low	11	6	5		
POWER					
High	10	3	7		
Moderate	11	7	4	3.30	N.S.
Low	9	6	3		

N.S. = not significant at .10 level

NOTES

[1] The maximum possible score for one story is 11 for achievement; 7 for affiliation; and 11 for power. In this study a six story set of pictures was used.

[2] Joseph Veroff, et al., "The Use of Thematic Apperception to Assess Motivation in a Nation-wide Interview Study." *Psychological Monographs,* 1960, 94 (12, Whole No. 499).

[3] In comparing the differences between the two means, the use of Z test is more appropriate especially when the sample size is more than thirty.

[4] In comparing the differences between the two means, especially when the sample size is thirty or less, the use of the student's t-test is more appropriate in evaluating statistical results.

CHAPTER V

DISCUSSION AND CONCLUSIONS

The objectives of this study were: (1) to assess the achievement, affiliation, and power motives of women managers; and (2) to determine the extent to which these motives were related to their preferences for male or female superior, subordinates, and co-workers, and to other demographic variables.

The results of this study were reported in Chapter IV. This chapter contains: (1) a discussion of the results; (2) limitations of the study; (3) implication; (4) some suggestions for future research; and (5) a summary of the study.

Discussion of Results

Achievement Motive. The present study clearly indicates that women managers have a higher need for achievement than was found for women in general as reported in Veroff's study.[1] In this respect, "today's management woman" is markedly different from women in the general population. However, it must be noted that the national sample data (Veroff's study) on women were obtained sixteen years ago and are the only data available to make any comparisons. The last fifteen years have seen an extraordinary change in the role of women. Women are getting more education, are seeking managerial jobs, and engaging in more direct competition with men in the job market. The results of this study indicated that women managers, like men managers, are strongly motivated to achieve and are concerned with getting ahead. That is why, perhaps, these women have chosen to go into management which has been a traditionally male dominated profession. Furthermore, high achievement motive in women managers may reflect a desire or drive to satisfy their needs for self-esteem.

This research also presents evidence that women managers employed in the manufacturing sector have a higher need for achievement than women managers employed in the service sector. Individuals differ widely in their reason for selecting various careers and occupations. A review of the literature on achievement motive discussed in Chapter II indicates that people with high need for achievement are likely to be attracted to occupations which provide independence, challenge, a sense of accomplishment, creativeness, and performance feedback. This suggests that the selection of occupation or career is dictated to some degree by the individual motives. It appears that women managers with high achievement needs seek out occupations in the manufacturing sector because they believe the manufacturing environment provides a greater degree of challenge, growth, and independence than the service sector. Furthermore, the relative ease with which performance is measured in manufacturing organizations provides greater opportunity for feedback on performance for self appraisal. The service sector, on the other hand, is typified by a "cooperative" environment where the emphasis is relatively strong on social interaction and feedback on performance is more difficult to generate. Therefore, such an environment may not be compatible with the profile of a high achiever.

Affiliation Motive. The research found no significant differences in the level of affiliation motive of women managers and women in general.[2] One possible explanation would be that women managers have a desire to maintain the traditional values of love, affection, and personal relationship. This interpretation is consistent with the viewpoint of Stein and Bailey who suggest that "attainment of excellence is often a goal of females' achievement efforts, but the areas in which such attainment is sought are frequently social skills and other areas perceived as feminine."[3] A second interpretation may be their desire to achieve acceptance and effective interpersonal relationships with the people with whom they work because it is perceived to be an important aspect of a manager's job. It was also found that women managers employed in the service sector have a higher need for affiliation than women managers employed in the manufacturing sector. The results suggest that women managers with high need for affiliation are attracted to occupations where there is a high degree of social contact. The role of a woman manager in the service sector (banks, utilities, etc.) requires social interaction with workers as well as with customers. Second, the environment in the service sector emphasizes "cooperation" rather than "competition" by providing stronger job security than is found in the manufacturing sector. This implies that social interaction and cooperative effort are perceived by the managers as "acceptable standards." Organizations use these standards as a criterion for rewards. Therefore, women managers with a high need for affiliation are motivated to achieve or accomplish such standards.

Power Motive. The results indicate that women managers have a higher need for power than women in general.[4] "Since managers are primarily concerned with influencing others, it seems obvious that they should be characterized by a high need for power."[5] This viewpoint, therefore, is consistent with the findings of this study. In his research on the power motive of female students, Winter reported that women's interests in getting power are as strong as men's interests.[6] The results of this study agree with this statement. The present results also indicate that women managers employed in manufacturing have a higher need for power than women managers employed in the service sector. One possible explanation for the variation in scores would be that women managers employed in manufacturing are more concerned with influencing and convincing others in order to resolve organizational conflicts. It must also be pointed out that managers in the manufacturing sector had more years of managerial experience in the organization. This may have accounted for (or be a result of) their high need for power.

The overall results on achievement, affiliation, and power indicate that women managers are significantly different in their need for achievement and power from women in the general population. Their need for affiliation, however, was not significantly different from that of women in general. A comparative analysis of the three motives between the two groups, managers employed in manufacturing and service, yielded some significant differences.

The results obtained from this study on women managers cannot be compared with those found in studies on male managers. However, motive patterns of men and women managers can be compared. The motive profile of men and women managers is illustrated in Figure 5.1. The motive pattern of women managers for the entire sample and for the managers employed in the service sector is somewhat different from men managers. However, the motive profile of women managers employed in the manufacturing sector closely resembles that of men managers. This suggests that women managers employed in the manufacturing sector are quite similar to men managers with respect to motives. As more women enter the management profession, these motive patterns may become identical.

Relationship Between Motives and Preference for Male or Female Superior, Subordinates, and Co-workers. Eighty percent of the entire sample preferred a male over a female supervisor. The results indicate no significant relationship between the motives (high, moderate, and low) and preference for supervisor's sex. However, preference for subordinate's sex was found to be related to motives. Women managers with a high need for achievement, a high need for power, and a low need for affiliation preferred male over female subordinates. Women managers with a low need for achievement and moderate and low need for power preferred the female subordinate. No significant relationship was found between the motives and preference for co-workers' sex. For managers employed in manufacturing, the achievement motive was found to be related to their preference for supervisor's sex. High need achievers as well as low need achievers preferred a male supervisor, whereas moderate need achievers were evenly divided in their preference for supervisor's sex. But the relatively small sample size makes it difficult to draw any strong conclusions. The results did not indicate any significant relationship between the motives and preference for male or female subordinates or co-workers. For managers employed in the service sector, there was no significant relationship between the three motives and preference for the sex of their supervisor, subordinate,

FIGURE 5.1

MEAN SCORES

	McClelland*	Total Sample	Manufacturing	Service
nAch	6.74	6.53	7.58	5.43
nAff	2.63	5.45	3.52	7.50
nPow	6.30	3.97	5.10	2.80

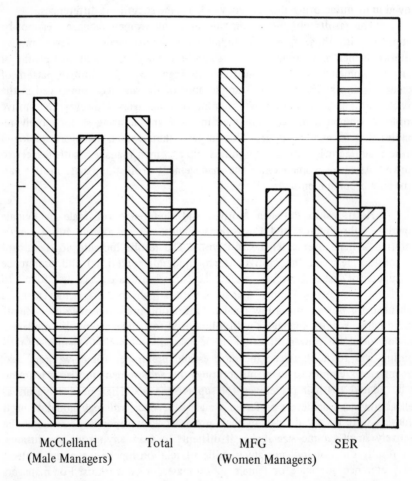

| McClelland | Total | MFG | SER |
| (Male Managers) | | (Women Managers) | |

* David C. McClelland, *The Achieving Society*. Princeton: Van Nostrand, 1961, p. 498.

or co-worker. However, the overall data tend to suggest that they are more likely to prefer a male supervisor, female subordinates, and female co-workers.

The overall results of this study regarding their preference for a male supervisor are consistent with the findings of pollster Louis Harris.[7] The Louis Harris poll found that women prefer a male boss to a female boss by a margin of 8 to 1. Lack of confidence in the managerial ability of their own sex was accounted for their favorable attitudes toward a male supervisor. Due to the relative scarcity of women managers near the top of the managerial hierarchy, women may be inexperienced in terms of their working relationships with a female boss. The increasing participation of women in management jobs may in the future reflect a different trend. In the next decade or two, as more women are promoted into the upper managerial level, lower level women managers may gain more confidence in the ability of female supervisors. Certainly they will gain more experience in working with female superiors.

In this culture men are perceived as achievers, and achievers prefer to be associated with achievers.[8] This may be the reason that women managers with a high need for achievement, a high need for power, and a low need for affiliation prefer male subordinates. Certain selected occupations, especially production and manufacturing, still tend to be male dominated. The results for the service sector indicated that women managers prefer to be associated with female subordinates and female co-workers. In the service sector, women are culturally trained to work with their own sex and have had considerable opportunity to develop satisfactory working relationships.

Relationships Between Motives and Other Variables. Although the results did not indicate any relationships between motives and reasons for organizational preference, it was found that women managers are more likely to rate "challenge" and "growth" as the most important elements of their job. This finding is consistent with various other studies done on motivation. Herzberg has reported that managers are primarily motivated by "satisfiers."[9] His list of satisfiers include growth and challenge.

The achievement, affiliation, and power motives of the entire sample were found to be unrelated to education. The only exception was the data on women managers employed in the manufacturing sector; high need for achievement was related to college education. Furthermore, an analysis of data of managers who scored high in any of the three motives indicates that the percentage of subjects (total subjects and the subjects employed in manufacturing) scoring above the median with college education is higher than the percentage of high scorers with high school education. Veroff's results for women in general are similar.[10] However, in the service sector, the percentage of managers scoring high in any of the three motives with high school education was substantially higher than the percentage of high scorers with college education. These results suggest that the subjects from the two industrial sectors have different perspectives with respect to education. Perhaps the managers employed in the manufacturing sector place high value on higher education in order to improve, to gain recognition, to compete, to move up the ladder, and to be well informed with respect to the new developments in business and technology. It is, of course, possible that the manufacturing sector places more emphasis on education when hiring and promoting employees. This would make the higher educational level of women managers in manufacturing a result rather than a cause.

It was found that women managers high in need for achievement and need for affiliation were younger (under 40). Again Veroff reports similar results.[11] However, Veroff's results indicate that the power motive was highest in the younger age group (21 to 34), while the present study found the power motive strongest in the older group (40 and over). One possible explanation is the amount of time older women have been associated with management in industry. Experience in managerial positions and the opportunity to influence and control the behavior and actions of subordinates is, if the woman manager is skilled, associated with high rewards. Younger women, unexposed to wielding managerial power, are less likely to have such high need for power. This explanation is consistent with the findings of the present study that women managers with more years of managerial experience showed a higher need for power than those with less experience.

The overall results on income and the motives indicate that managers with high incomes ($15,000 and over) scored high in any one of the three motives. It was also found that women managers with a high need for affiliation and employed in the service sector tended to earn more income than others; however, the relatively small sample size makes it difficult to draw any strong conclusions. No significant relationships were found between the motives and the marital status of women managers.

One interesting result was the relationship between smoking and the achievement motive. The results indicate that women managers high in need achievement are less likely to smoke than others. This may possibly suggest that high need achievers are less likely to take high risks which may be hazardous, which is consistent with the characteristics associated with the achievement motive. Individuals with high need for achievement prefer to take moderate risks.[12]

Relationship Between Motives. The results indicate that women managers' need for achievement is positively related to power motive and the power motive is negatively related to affiliation motive. Bowen in his review of the literature on the relationship between the three needs also found similar results. However, the results were based on male samples.[13] One possible explanation would be that the subjects of this study and male subjects (studies reviewed by Bowen) seem to possess somewhat similar characteristics. It is also possible that women managers, like men managers while strongly motivated to achieve are also concerned with influencing and convincing others. Bowen also states that:

> A second generalization suggested by the data surveyed is that there is a distinct shortage of studies of women. If more data on women were available, it would be useful in evaluating a possible sex difference in the correlations between nAch and nAff which tend to be negative for men and positive for women. Confirmation of such a finding would be consistent with sex roles which emphasize achievement through nurturance and support for women while defining such effeminate traits as signs of weakness for men.[14]

The results of this study do not support Bowen's argument. The relationship between nAch and nAff is not positive but not significant. Additional research on women is needed to draw any strong conclusions.

Limitations of the Study

While the sample size used in this research is similar to other studies of this type, it is not large and the results must be interpreted with caution. First, the present sample may not be representative of the total population. Second, comparison of these results with those found in studies on male managers is risky because two different sets of test forms (female and male sets of pictures) are used. These limitations, however, do not invalidate the findings reported here.

Implications

The results of this study strongly suggest that the present and the prospective employers should make a sincere effort to understand the motivational characteristics of women managers. Certain jobs require achievement behavior while other jobs may require affiliation or power behavior. For example, managers with a high need for achievement can be assigned to tasks requiring challenge, individual responsibility, creativity, and some degree of risk taking, whereas managers with a high need for affiliation can be assigned to jobs which require social interaction. By identifying the need patterns of potential managers, organizations can make appropriate decisions in selecting personnel.

Moreover, organizations, by understanding the motive patterns of their managers, can develop training programs to arouse various motives. Such training programs can help managers understand their own motive profile and behaviors associated with the motives. This can be accomplished by means of simulated games, exercise, and management development courses. By participating in these programs, managers can examine their needs, behavior, and the impact of various motives on job performance.

McClelland and his associates have instituted training programs to develop the achievement motive. According to McClelland, the achievement motive "can be developed by certain special training techniques, just the way a language skill can be acquired in adulthood." The special training methods emphasize: setting realistic and specific goals; learning how to think and behave like a high achievement individual; understanding the self (need structure); and emotional support by the trainer for developing motive.[15]

Such training programs conducted on executives in the United States and other countries have proved to be effective in increasing the level of achievement motive.[16] Similar methods could be used to develop affiliation and power motives.

This process will help management examine and understand the differences in motives of their managers and will lead to better management by establishing specific criteria for the selection, placement, training, and career development. Furthermore, this will not only help the psychological and mental growth of the manager but will also provide a better fit between the individual and the organizational requirements.

Suggestions for Future Research

The research evidence obtained from this study strongly suggests the importance of future research in the areas defined below. More data are needed to understand the motivational patterns of women managers; therefore, it is recommended that future research include a large sample of women managers.

Future research should also consider including women managers occupying different levels of managerial positions as well as staff and line managers. This will help identify any relationship between motives and the level of position occupied by the managers.

To determine the similarities and differences in the motive profiles of male and female managers in the manufacturing and service sector, it is suggested that new research should be conducted on male and female managers.

As the organizations tend to employ and integrate more women, blacks, and other minorities in the managerial group, it is important that future research should include such groups. Specific research should be made to compare the need structure of black and white women managers.

Various studies on males have looked into the relationship between motives and job performance; however, there are no available studies on women. Therefore, future research should investigate any possible relationship between motives and job performance of women managers.

Few longitudinal studies conducted on male college educated students have reported a positive relationship between motives and career selection. However, such studies using female students are limited. Currently there is a tremendous increase in the number of women seeking admission to professional business schools and colleges. This increase in enrollment of women in colleges warrants a longitudinal study to determine if certain motives lead to certain career choices.

Future research should also consider using women managers employed in government, various social and other non-profit organizations. Additional research is also needed to explore the impact of age, education, and marital status on the motives.

The increased participation of women, blacks, and other minority groups in the management will require substantial interaction between male and female, white and black, and other minority groups. The present TAT method, by requiring different sets of pictures for different groups, makes it impossible to compare the motive scores between men and women, black and white and other minority groups. It is strongly recommended that researchers investigate the feasibility of developing a standardized set of pictures which will make it possible to compare the motive scores of different groups.

To determine if traditional stereotypes still exist among male managers, future research should look into the male manager's perception of female managers. Consideration should also be given to reinvestigating the female manager's perception of female and male superiors, subordinates, and co-workers.

Summary

The objective of this study was to determine the achievement, affiliation, and power motive of women managers. The results of this study have provided a partial understanding of the motivational characteristics of women managers.

Two major conclusions are supported by the results of this study. First, women managers are significantly different from women in general in their need for achievement and power. Second, women managers' need for affiliation is not significantly different from women managers employed in the service sector in their needs for achievement, affiliation, and power.

96   DISCUSSION AND CONCLUSIONS

NOTES

[1] Joseph Veroff, et al., "The Use of Thematic Apperception to Assess Motivation in a Nationwide Interview Study." *Psychological Monographs,* 1960, 74 (Whole No. 499).

[2] *Ibid.*

[3] A.H. Stein and M.M. Bailey, "The Socialization of Achievement Orientation in Females." *Psychological Bulletin,* 1973, 80, p. 363.

[4] Veroff, et al., *loc. cit.*

[5] David C. McClelland, "The Two Faces of Power." *Journal of International Affairs,* 1970, 24, p. 31.

[6] David G. Winter, "Power Motives and Power Behavior in Women." Paper presented at the American Psychological Convention, Chicago, 1975.

[7] Louis Harris and Associates, *The Virginia Slims American Women's Opinion Poll.* New York, 1971.

[8] E.G. French, "Motivation as a Variable in Work Partner Selection," *Journal of Abnormal and Social Psychology,* 1956, 53, pp. 96-99.

[9] Frederick Herzberg, et al., *The Motivation to Work.* New York: John Wiley and Sons, 1959.

[10] Veroff, et al., *loc. cit.*

[11] *Ibid.*

[12] David C. McClelland, "Business Drive and National Achievement." *Harvard Business Review,* July-August 1962, pp. 98-112.

[13] Donald D. Bowen, "Reported Patterns in TAT Measures of Needs for Achievement, Affiliation, and Power." *Journal of Personality Assessment,* 1973, 37, pp. 424-430.

[14] *Ibid.,* p. 429.

[15] David C. McClelland,"Achievement Motive Can Be Developed."*Harvard Business Review,* 1965, 43, pp. 6-24.

[16] *Ibid.*

APPENDIX A

DEMOGRAPHIC AND OTHER RESEARCH RELATED DATA

TABLE A.1
AGE GROUPING OF SUBJECTS

AGE	Total Sample		Subjects Employed in Manufacturing Sector		Subjects Employed in Service Sector	
	Number of Subjects	Percent of Subjects	Number of Subjects	Percent of Subjects	Number of Subjects	Percent of Subjects
0 to 25	5	8.2	3	9.7	2	6.7
26 to 32	21	34.4	7	22.6	14	46.7
33 to 39	9	14.8	5	16.1	4	13.3
40 to 46	10	16.4	8	25.8	2	6.7
47 to 53	9	14.8	4	12.9	5	16.7
54 and over	7	11.5	4	12.9	3	10.0
Total	61	100.0	31	100.0	30	100.0

TABLE A.2
MARITAL STATUS OF SUBJECTS

MARITAL STATUS	Total Sample		Subjects Employed in Manufacturing Sector		Subjects Employed in Service Sector	
	Number of Subjects	Percent of Subjects	Number of Subjects	Percent of Subjects	Number of Subjects	Percent of Subjects
Single	18	29.5	9	29.0	9	30.0
Married	37	60.7	19	61.3	18	60.0
Engaged	1	1.6	1	3.2	0	0.0
Divorced	3	4.9	1	3.2	2	6.7
Widowed	2	3.3	1	3.2	1	3.3
Total	61	100.0	31	100.0	30	100.0

TABLE A.3
EDUCATIONAL LEVEL OF SUBJECTS

EDUCATION	Total Sample		Subjects Employed in Manufacturing Sector		Subjects Employed in Service Sector	
	Number of Subjects	Percent of Subjects	Number of Subjects	Percent of Subjects	Number of Subjects	Percent of Subjects
Some High School	1	1.6	1	3.2	0	0.0
High School Graduate	16	26.2	10	32.3	6	20.0
Some College	24	39.3	10	32.3	14	46.7
College Graduate	13	21.3	5	16.1	8	26.7
Master's & Ph.D.	7	11.5	5	16.1	2	6.7
Total	61	100.0	31	100.0	30	100.0

TABLE A.4
INCOME LEVEL OF SUBJECTS

INCOME	Total Sample		Subjects Employed in Manufacturing Sector		Subjects Employed in Service Sector	
	Number of Subjects	Percent of Subjects	Number of Subjects	Percent of Subjects	Number of Subjects	Percent of Subjects
0 to 9,999	4	6.6	2	6.5	2	6.7
10,000 to 14,999	27	44.3	14	45.2	13	43.3
15,000 to 19,999	19	31.1	12	38.7	7	23.3
20,000 to 24,999	8	13.1	1	3.2	7	23.3
25,000 and over	3	4.9	2	6.5	1	3.3
Total	61	100.0	31	100.0	30	100.0

TABLE A.5
JOB POSITION OF SUBJECTS

JOB TITLE	Total Sample		Subjects Employed in Manufacturing Sector		Subjects Employed in Service Sector	
	Number of Subjects	Percent of Subjects	Number of Subjects	Percent of Subjects	Number of Subjects	Percent of Subjects
Director	3	4.9	2	6.5	1	3.3
Manager	23	37.7	10	32.3	13	43.3
Supervisor	33	54.1	17	54.8	16	53.3
Professional	2	3.3	2	6.5	0	0.0
Total	61	100.0	31	100.0	30	100.0

TABLE A.6
YEARS IN MANAGERIAL POSITION

YEARS IN MANAGERIAL POSITION	Total Sample		Subjects Employed in Manufacturing Sector		Subjects Employed in Service Sector	
	Number of Subjects	Percent of Subjects	Number of Subjects	Percent of Subjects	Number of Subjects	Percent of Subjects
1 to 3	37	60.7	21	67.7	16	53.3
4 to 7	15	24.6	7	22.6	8	26.7
7 to 10	5	8.2	2	6.5	3	10.0
11 and over	4	6.5	1	3.2	3	10.0
Total	61	100.0	31	100.0	30	100.0

TABLE A.7
JOB PROMOTIONS RECEIVED IN THE LAST FIVE YEARS

PROMOTIONS	Total Sample		Subjects Employed in Manufacturing Sector		Subjects Employed in Service Sector	
	Number of Subjects	Percent of Subjects	Number of Subjects	Precent of Subjects	Number of Subjects	Percent of Subjects
None	5	8.2	2	6.5	3	10.0
One	20	32.8	13	41.9	7	23.3
Two	22	36.1	10	32.3	12	40.0
Three	11	18.0	4	12.8	7	23.3
Four	1	1.6	0	0.0	1	3.4
Five and over	2	3.3	2	6.5	0	0.0
Total	61	100.0	31	100.0	30	100.0

TABLE A.8
SUPERVISOR'S SEX

SUPERVISOR'S SEX	Total Sample		Subjects Employed in Manufacturing Sector		Subjects Employed in Service Sector	
	Number of Subjects	Percent of Subjects	Number of Subjects	Percent of Subjects	Number of Subjects	Percent of Subjects
Female	9	15.0	0	0.0	9	30.0
Male	52	85.0	31	100.0	21	70.0
Total	61	100.0	31	100.0	30	100.00

TABLE A.9
SUBORDINATES (IMMEDIATE)

NUMBER OF SUBORDINATES	Total Sample		Subjects Employed in Manufacturing Sector		Subjects Employed in Service Sector	
	Number of Subjects	Percent of Subjects	Number of Subjects	Percent of Subjects	Number of Subjects	Percent of Subjects
0 to 3	32	52.5	11	35.5	21	70.0
4 to 6	29	47.5	20	64.5	9	30.0
7 and over	0	0.0	0	0.0	0	0.0
Total	61	100.0	31	100.0	30	100.0
Median		3.42		3.73		3.04

TABLE A.10
CO-WORKERS

NUMBER OF CO-WORKERS	Total Sample		Subjects Employed in Manufacturing Sector		Subjects Employed in Service Sector	
	Number of[a] Subjects	Percent of Subjects	Number of[b] Subjects	Percent of Subjects	Number of[c] Subjects	Percent of Subjects
0 to 3	36	66.7	19	76.0	17	58.6
4 to 6	18	33.3	6	24.0	12	41.4
7 and over	0	0.0	0	0.0	0	0.0
Total	54	100.0	25	100.0	29	100.0
Median	2.81		2.57		3.1	

a indicates that seven subjects did not respond to this question
b indicates that six subjects did not respond to this question
c indicates that one subject did not respond to this question

TABLE A.11
MOST IMPORTANT SUBORDINATE

IMPORTANT SUBORDINATE	Total Sample		Subjects Employed in Manufacturing Sector		Subjects Employed in Service Sector	
	Number of[a] Subjects	Percent of Subjects	Number of[b] Subjects	Percent of Subjects	Number of Subjects	Percent of Subjects
Female	34	58.6	14	45.2	20	74.1
Male	24	41.4	17	54.8	7	25.9
Total	58	100.0	31	100.0	27	100.0

[a] indicates that three subjects did not respond to the question
[b] indicates that three subjects did not respond to the question

TABLE A.12
MOST IMPORTANT CO-WORKER

IMPORTANT CO-WORKER	Total Sample		Subjects Employed in Manufacturing Sector		Subjects Employed in Service Sector	
	Number of [a] Subjects	Percent of Subjects	Number of [b] Subjects	Percent of Subjects	Number of [c] Subjects	Percent of Subjects
Female	20	38.5	7	29.2	13	46.4
Male	32	61.5	17	70.8	15	53.6
Total	52	100.0	24	100.0	28	100.0

[a] indicates that nine subjects did not respond to the question
[b] indicates that seven subjects did not respond to the question
[c] indicates that two subjects did not respond to the question

TABLE A.13
PREFERENCE FOR SUPERVISOR'S SEX

PREFERENCE FOR SUPERVISOR	Total Sample		Subjects Employed in Manufacturing Sector		Subjects Employed in Service Sector	
	Number of Subjects	Percent of Subjects	Number of Subjects	Percent of Subjects	Number of Subjects	Percent of Subjects
Female	12	19.7	3	9.7	9	30.0
Male	49	80.3	28	90.3	21	70.0
Total	61	100.0	31	100.0	30	100.0

TABLE A.14
PREFERENCE FOR SUBORDINATE'S SEX

PREFERENCE FOR SUBORDINATE	Total Sample		Subjects Employed in Manufacturing Sector		Subjects Employed in Service Sector	
	Number of Subjects	Percent of Subjects	Number of Subjects	Percent of Subjects	Number of Subjects	Percent of Subjects
Female	31	50.8	10	32.3	21	70.0
Male	30	49.2	21	67.7	9	30.0
Total	61	100.0	31	100.0	30	100.0

TABLE A.15
PREFERENCE FOR CO-WORKER'S SEX

PREFERENCE FOR CO-WORKER	Total Sample		Subjects Employed in Manufacturing Sector		Subjects Employed in Service Sector	
	Number of[a] Subjects	Percent of Subjects	Number of[b] Subjects	Percent of Subjects	Number of Subjects	Percent of Subjects
Female	33	56.9	15	53.6	18	60.0
Male	25	43.1	13	46.4	12	40.0
Total	58	100.0	28	100.0	30	100.0

[a] indicates that three subjects did not respond to this question
[b] indicates that three subjects did not respond to this question

TABLE A.16
REASONS FOR ORGANIZATIONAL PREFERENCE

ORGANIZATIONAL PREFERENCE	Total Sample		Subjects Employed in Manufacturing Sector		Subjects Employed in Service Sector	
	Number of Subjects	Percent of Subjects	Number of Subjects	Percent of Subjects	Number of Subjects	Percent of Subjects
Stability	7	11.5	3	9.6	4	13.3
Challenge	38	62.5	18	58.1	20	66.7
Salary	4	6.6	2	6.5	2	6.7
Growth	9	14.8	6	19.3	3	10.0
Social Responsibility	3	4.9	2	6.5	1	3.3
Total	61	100.0	31	100.0	30	100.0

TABLE A.17
ORDER OF BIRTH

ORDER OF BIRTH	Total Sample		Subjects Employed in Manufacturing Sector		Subjects Employed in Service Sector	
	Number of Subjects	Percent of Subjects	Number of Subjects	Percent of Subjects	Number of Subjects	Percent of Subjects
First born child	21	34.4	11	35.5	10	33.3
Second born child	12	19.7	7	22.6	5	16.7
Third born child	13	21.3	7	22.6	6	20.0
Fourth born child	6	9.8	2	6.4	4	13.3
Fifth born and over	9	14.8	4	12.9	5	16.7
Total	61	100.0	31	100.0	30	100.0

TABLE A.18
PARENT'S EDUCATION (MOTHER)

MOTHER'S EDUCATION	Total Sample		Subjects Employed in Manufacturing Sector		Subjects Employed in Service Sector	
	Number of [a] Subjects	Percent of Subjects	Number of Subjects	Percent of Subjects	Number of [b] Subjects	Percent of Subjects
Some High School	26	43.3	15	48.4	11	37.9
High School Graduate	28	46.7	12	38.7	16	55.2
Some College	5	8.3	3	9.7	2	6.9
College Graduate	1	1.7	1	3.2	0	0.0
Master's & Ph.D.	0	0.0	0	0.0	0	0.0
Total	60	100.0	31	100.0	29	100.0

[a] indicates that one subject did not respond to the question
[b] indicates that one subject did not respond to the question

TABLE A.19
PARENT'S EDUCATION (FATHER)

FATHER'S EDUCATION	Total Sample		Subjects Employed in Manufacturing Sector		Subjects Employed in Service Sector	
	Number of [a] Subjects	Percent of Subjects	Number of [b] Subjects	Percent of Subjects	Number of [c] Subjects	Percent of Subjects
Some High School	22	38.6	11	39.3	11	38.0
High School Graduate	24	42.1	12	42.8	12	41.4
Some College	4	7.0	1	3.6	3	10.3
College Graduate	7	12.3	4	14.3	3	10.3
Master's & Ph.D.	0	0.0	0	0.0	0	0.0
Total	57	100.0	28	100.0	29	100.0

[a] indicates that four subjects did not respond to the question
[b] indicates that three subjects did not respond to the question
[c] indicates that one subject did not respond to the question

TABLE A.20
PARENT'S OCCUPATION (MOTHER)

MOTHER'S OCCUPATION	Total Sample		Subjects Employed in Manufacturing Sector		Subjects Employed in Service Sector	
	Number of[a] Subjects	Percent of Subjects	Number of Subjects	Percent of Subjects	Number of[b] Subjects	Percent of Subjects
Clerical or Sales	8	13.3	2	6.5	6	20.7
Craftsman or Foreman (farming, factory workers, etc)	6	10.0	4	12.9	2	6.9
Professional & Technical (manager, doctor, lawyer, etc)	3	5.0	2	6.5	1	3.4
Housewife	40	66.7	22	71.0	18	62.1
Own Business	3	5.0	1	3.1	2	6.9
Total	60	100.0	31	100.0	29	100.0

a indicates that one subject did not respond to the question
b indicates that one subject did not respond to the question

TABLE A.21
PARENT'S OCCUPATION (FATHER)

FATHER'S OCCUPATION	Total Sample		Subjects Employed in Manufacturing Sector		Subjects Employed in Service Sector	
	Number of [a] Subjects	Percent of Subjects	Number of Subjects	Percent of Subjects	Number of [b] Subjects	Percent of Subjects
Clerical or Sales	5	8.3	1	3.2	4	13.8
Craftsman or Foreman (farming, factory worker, etc)	38	63.3	21	67.7	17	58.6
Professional & Technical (manager, doctor, lawyer, etc)	7	11.7	4	12.9	3	10.3
Own Business	10	16.7	5	16.2	5	17.3
Total	60	100.0	31	100.0	29	100.0

[a] indicates that one subject did not respond to the question
[b] indicates that one subject did not respond to the question

TABLE A.22
CONSUMPTION OF ALCOHOL

CONSUMPTION OF ALCOHOL	Total Sample		Subjects Employed in Manufacturing Sector		Subjects Employed in Service Sector	
	Number of Subjects	Percent of Subjects	Number of Subjects	Percent of Subjects	Number of Subjects	Percent of Subjects
Yes	48	78.7	23	74.2	25	83.3
No	13	21.3	8	25.8	5	16.7
Total	61	100.0	31	100.0	30	100.0

TABLE A.23
CONSUMPTION OF ALCOHOL – HOW OFTEN [a]

HOW OFTEN	Total Sample		Subjects Employed in Manufacturing Sector		Subjects Employed in Service Sector	
	Number of Subjects	Percent of Subjects	Number of Subjects	Percent of Subjects	Number of Subjects	Percent of Subjects
Daily	2	4.0	1	4.2	1	4.0
During Weekends	4	8.2	0	0.0	4	16.0
Socially	19	38.8	9	37.5	10	40.0
Occasionally	24	49.0	14	58.3	10	40.0
Total	49	100.0	24	100.0	25	100.0

[a] includes subjects who consumed alcohol

TABLE A.24
SMOKING

SMOKING	Total Sample		Subjects Employed in Manufacturing Sector		Subjects Employed in Service Sector	
	Number of Subjects	Percent of Subjects	Number of Subjects	Percent of Subjects	Number of Subjects	Percent of Subjects
Yes	21	34.4	11	35.5	10	33.3
No	40	65.6	20	64.5	20	66.7
Total	61	100.0	31	100.0	30	100.0

TABLE A.25
SMOKING – HOW MUCH[a]

HOW MUCH	Total Sample		Subjects Employed in Manufacturing Sector		Subjects Employed in Service Sector	
	Number of Subjects	Percent of Subjects	Number of Subjects	Percent of Subjects	Number of Subjects	Percent of Subjects
Less than a pack a day	9	42.9	3	27.3	6	60.0
One pack a day	7	33.3	5	45.5	2	20.0
Two packs a day	5	23.8	3	27.2	2	20.0
Three and over	0	0.0	0	0.0	0	0.0
Total	21	100.0	11	100.0	10	100.0

a   includes subjects who smoke

TABLE A.26
ACHIEVEMENT SCORES

SCORES	Total Sample		Subjects Employed in Manufacturing Sector		Subjects Employed in Service Sector	
	Number of Subjects	Percent of Subjects	Number of Subjects	Percent of Subjects	Number of Subjects	Percent of Subjects
0	2	3.3	0	0.0	2	6.7
1	7	11.5	4	12.9	3	10.0
2	3	4.9	2	6.5	1	3.3
3	1	1.6	0	0.0	1	3.3
4	9	14.8	4	12.9	5	16.7
5	5	8.2	3	9.7	2	6.7
6	7	11.5	1	3.2	6	20.0
7	6	9.8	1	3.2	5	16.7
8	3	4.9	3	9.7	0	0.0
9	2	3.3	0	0.0	2	6.7
10	2	3.3	1	3.2	1	3.3

Continued....

TABLE A.26
ACHIEVEMENT SCORES

(continued)

SCORES	Total Sample		Subjects Employed in Manufacturing Sector		Subjects Employed in Service Sector	
	Number of Subjects	Percent of Subjects	Number of Subjects	Percent of Subjects	Number of Subjects	Percent of Subjects
11	5	8.2	5	16.1	0	0.0
12	1	1.6	1	3.2	0	0.0
13	6	9.8	4	12.9	2	6.7
14	1	1.6	1	3.2	0	0.0
15	0	0.0	0	0.0	0	0.0
16	1	1.6	1	3.2	0	0.0
Total	61	100.0	31	100.0	30	100.0
Mean	6.525		7.581		5.433	
Median	6.000		7.667		5.667	
S.D.	4.113		4.559		3.329	

TABLE A.27
AFFILIATION SCORES

SCORES	Total Sample		Subjects Employed in Manufacturing Sector		Subjects Employed in Service Sector	
	Number of Subjects	Percent of Subjects	Number of Subjects	Percent of Subjects	Number of Subjects	Percent of Subjects
0	2	3.3	2	6.5	0	0.0
1	1	1.6	1	3.2	0	0.0
2	11	18.0	10	32.3	1	3.3
3	6	9.8	6	19.4	0	0.0
4	9	14.8	4	12.9	5	16.7
5	9	14.8	4	12.9	5	16.7
6	2	3.3	1	3.2	1	3.3
7	5	8.2	1	3.2	4	13.3
8	3	4.9	1	3.2	2	6.7
9	2	3.3	0	0.0	2	6.7
10	5	8.2	0	0.0	5	16.7

Continued....

(continued)

TABLE A.27
AFFILIATION SCORES

SCORES	Total Sample		Subjects Employed in Manufacturing Sector		Subjects Employed in Service Sector	
	Number of Subjects	Percent of Subjects	Number of Subjects	Percent of Subjects	Number of Subjects	Percent of Subjects
11	3	4.9	0	0.0	3	10.0
12	1	1.6	0	0.0	1	3.3
13	1	1.6	1	3.2	0	0.0
14	0	0.0	0	0.0	0	0.0
15	1	1.6	0	0.0	1	3.3
Total	61	100.0	31	100.0	30	100.0
Mean	5.475		3.516		7.50	
Median	4.667		2.917		7.25	
S.D.	3.443		2.541		3.082	

TABLE A.28
POWER SCORES

SCORES	Total Sample		Subjects Employed in Manufacturing Sector		Subjects Employed in Service Sector	
	Number of Subjects	Percent of Subjects	Number of Subjects	Percent of Subjects	Number of Subjects	Percent of Subjects
0	8	13.1	2	6.5	6	20.0
1	5	8.2	2	6.5	3	10.0
2	6	9.8	2	6.5	4	13.3
3	9	14.8	2	6.5	7	23.3
4	11	18.0	7	22.6	4	13.3
5	6	9.8	3	9.7	3	10.0
6	5	8.2	3	9.7	2	6.7
7	4	6.6	4	12.9	0	0.0
8	2	3.3	2	6.5	0	0.0

Continued....

TABLE A.28
POWER SCORES

(continued)

SCORES	Total Sample		Subjects Employed in Manufacturing Sector		Subjects Employed in Service Sector	
	Number of Subjects	Percent of Subjects	Number of Subjects	Percent of Subjects	Number of Subjects	Percent of Subjects
9	2	3.3	1	3.2	1	3.3
10	2	3.3	2	6.5	0	0.0
11	0	0.0	0	0.0	0	0.0
12	1	1.6	1	3.2	0	0.0
Total	61	100.0	31	100.0	30	100.0
Mean	3.967		5.097		2.80	
Median	3.727		4.667		2.786	
S.D.	2.846		2.982		2.188	

TABLE A.29
RELATIONSHIP BETWEEN MOTIVE CATEGORY AND CONSUMPTION OF ALCOHOL
(For the Service Sector, N = 30)

Motive Category	Consumption of Alcohol			Chi-square	Significance Level
	N	Yes	No		
ACHIEVEMENT					
High	5	3	2		
Moderate	18	15	3	3.60	N.S.
Low	7	7	0		
AFFILIATION					
High	10	9	1		
Moderate	9	9	0	5.19	.07
Low	11	7	4		
POWER					
High	10	7	3		
Moderate	11	9	2	3.09	.21
Low	9	9	0		

N.S. = not significant at .10 level

TABLE A.30

RELATIONSHIP BETWEEN MOTIVE CATEGORY AND SMOKING

(For the Total Sample, N = 61)

Motive Category	N	Smoke Yes	No	Chi-square	Significance Level
ACHIEVEMENT					
High	18	5	13		
Moderate	21	8	13	.51	N.S.
Low	22	8	14		
AFFILIATION					
High	16	5	11		
Moderate	25	10	15	.59	N.S.
Low	20	6	14		
POWER					
High	16	4	12		
Moderate	26	13	13	4.93	.08
Low	19	4	15		

N.S. = not significant at .10 level

TABLE A.31
RELATIONSHIP BETWEEN MOTIVE CATEGORY AND SMOKING
(For the Manufacturing Sector, N = 31)

Motive Category	N	Smoke		Chi-square	Significance Level
		Yes	No		
ACHIEVEMENT					
High	13	3	10		
Moderate	5	0	5	7.48	.02
Low	13	8	5		
AFFILIATION					
High	8	2	6		
Moderate	10	4	6	.52	N.S.
Low	13	5	8		
POWER					
High	10	1	9		
Moderate	13	7	6	4.77	.09
Low	8	3	5		

N.S. = not significant at .10 level

TABLE A.32

RELATIONSHIP BETWEEN MOTIVE CATEGORY AND THE DEGREE OF SMOKING

(For the Manufacturing Sector, N = 11)

Motive Category	N*	Less than one pack a day	One pack a day	Two packs a day	Chi-square	Significance
ACHIEVEMENT						
High	3	0	3	0		
Moderate	0	0	0	0	4.95	.08
Low	8	3	2	3		
AFFILIATION						
High	2	1	1	0		
Moderate	4	1	2	1	1.39	N.S.
Low	5	1	2	2		
POWER						
High	1	0	1	0		
Moderate	7	3	3	1	4.89	N.S.
Low	3	0	1	2		

* indicates does not include subjects who did not smoke

N.S. = not significant at .10 level

APPENDIX B

QUESTIONNAIRE

Please respond to the following questions to the best of your ability.

1. A. Which of the following type of organization do you prefer to work for? (check one)
    - (a) _____ Government
    - (b) _____ Retailing
    - (c) _____ Manufacturing
    - (d) _____ Service
    - (e) _____ Other_____

    B. What reasons characterize your above stated preference (check more than one)
    - (a) _____ Stability
    - (b) _____ Challenge
    - (c) _____ Salary
    - (d) _____ Growth
    - (e) _____ Social Responsibility

    C. Which of the above is most important? (check only one)
    - (a) _____ Stability
    - (b) _____ Challenge
    - (c) _____ Salary
    - (d) _____ Growth
    - (e) _____ Social Responsibility

2. Briefly state your title and nature of your position in the organization.
    - (a) Title _____
    - (b) Nature of Position _____
      _____

3. How long have you been in the managerial position?
    _____ year/years

4. How many job promotions have you received in the last five years? (circle the appropriate number)
    1 2 3 4 5 and more

5. My immediate supervisor is:
    - (a) _____ Female
    - (b) _____ Male

6. A. How many immediate subordinates do you have in your job?
        (Those who report directly to you)
        (a)   _____   1
        (b)   _____   2-3
        (c)   _____   4-6
        (d)   _____   7 and over
    B. Indicate how many immediate male & female subordinates you
        have in your job? (Fill in the correct number)
        (a)   _____   Female   (b)   _____   Male
    C. My most important subordinate is: (check only one)
        (a)   _____   Female   (b)   _____   Male
7. A. How many immediate co-workers do you have in your job?
        (a)   _____   1
        (b)   _____   2-3
        (c)   _____   4-6
        (d)   _____   7 and more
    B. Indicate how many immediate male & female co-workers you have.
        (Fill in the correct number)
        (a)   _____   Female   (b)   _____   Male
    C. My most important co-worker is: (check only one)
        (a)   _____   Female   (b)   _____   Male .
8. Which of the following relationships do you prefer in your job situation?
    A. Immediate Supervisor (check only one)
        (a)   _____   Male Supervisor
        (b)   _____   Female Supervisor
    B. Immediate Subordinate (check only one)
        (a)   _____   Male Subordinate
        (b)   _____   Female Subordinate
    C. Co-worker (check only one)
        (a)   _____   Male Co-worker
        (b)   _____   Female Co-worker
9. Do you consider performance feedback as an important element of your
    job?
    (a) _____ Yes
    (b) _____ No
10. Do you prefer to receive the performance feedback?
    (a) _____ Immediately after completing the assignment
    (b) _____ Some time after completing the assignment
    (c) _____ Does not matter when it is given

11. What magazines do you read or look at fairly regularly? (You can check more than one)
    (a) _____ Cosmopolitan and/or Vogue
    (b) _____ Playgirl and/or Penthouse
    (c) _____ Fortune and/or Business Week
    (d) _____ MS
    (e) _____ Ladies Home Journal
    (f) _____ Newsweek and/or Time
    (g) _____ People
    (h) _____ Good Housekeeping
    (i) _____ Other _____

12. Which of the following sports do you participate in?
    A. INDIVIDUAL
        (a) _____ Tennis
        (b) _____ Skiing
        (c) _____ Judo and/or Karate
        (d) _____ Golfing
    B. TEAM
        (a) _____ Basketball
        (b) _____ Bowling
        (c) _____ Volleyball
        (d) _____ Frisbee

13. Do you consume alcohol?
    (a) _____ Yes
    (b) _____ No
    If your answer is "yes," please answer the following:
    A. CONSUMPTION OF ALCOHOL
        (a) _____ daily
        (b) _____ during weekends
        (c) _____ socially
        (d) _____ occasionally
    B. TYPE OF ALCOHOL CONSUMED:
        (a) _____ Beer
        (b) _____ Mixed Drinks (Scotch & Water, Bloody Mary, etc.)
        (c) _____ Wine
        (d) _____ Straight Drinks (Scotch on the rocks, etc.)
        (e) _____ After Dinner Drink (Brandy, Liqueur, etc.)

14. Do you smoke?
    (a) _____ Yes
    (b) _____ No
    If your answer is "yes," please answer the following:

A. How much do you smoke?
   (a) _____ Less than a pack per day
   (b) _____ One pack per day
   (c) _____ Two packs per day
   (d) _____ Three packs per day
   (e) _____ More than three packs per day

DEMOGRAPHIC DATA

1. Age:
   - (a) _____ Less than 25
   - (b) _____ 26-32
   - (c) _____ 33-39
   - (d) _____ 40-46
   - (e) _____ 47-53
   - (f) _____ 54 and over
2. Marital Status:
   - (a) _____ Single
   - (b) _____ Married
   - (c) _____ Engaged
   - (d) _____ Divorced
   - (e) _____ Widowed
   - (f) _____ Living with Opposite Sex
3. Number of children (circle the number)
   1 2 3 4 5 6 and over
4. Number of brothers and sisters you have:
   (Fill in the correct numbers.)
   - (a) _____ Brothers (b) _____ Sisters
5. Your order of birth (circle the correct number):
   1 2 3 4 5 6th or over
6. Income (yours only)
   - (a) _____ Less than 9,999
   - (b) _____ 10,000 - 14,999
   - (c) _____ 15,000 - 19,999
   - (d) _____ 20,000 - 24,999
   - (e) _____ over 25,000
7. Education:

	YOURS	MOTHER'S	FATHER'S
(a) Some High School	_____	_____	_____
(b) High School Graduate	_____	_____	_____
(c) Some College	_____	_____	_____
(d) College Graduate	_____	_____	_____
(e) Graduate School (Master's & Ph.D.)	_____	_____	_____

8.   PARENT'S OCCUPATION: (If deceased or retired, what was their former occupation).

	MOTHER	FATHER
(a) Clerical or sales	_____	_____
(b) Craftsman or Foreman (Farming, Factory Workers, etc.)	_____	_____
(c) Professional & Technical (Manager, Doctor, Lawyer, etc.)	_____	_____
(d) Housewife	_____	_____
(e) Own Business	_____	_____

BIBLIOGRAPHY

Adler, Alfred. *Social Interest*. London: Faber and Faber, 1938.

American Heritage Dictionary. Boston, Massachusetts: Houghton Mifflin Company, 1973.

Anderson, Beverlee A., and W.J. McDowell. "The Corporate Women of Tomorrow: Personality and Attitudes." Unpublished paper, University of Cincinnati, 1976.

Andrews, J. "The Achievement Motive in Two Types of Organization." *Journal of Personality and Social Psychology*, 1967, 6, pp. 163-168.

Atkinson, J.W., R.W. Heyns, and J. Veroff. "The Effect of Experimental Arousal of the Affiliation Motive on Thematic Apperception." *Journal of Abnormal and Social Psychology*, 1954, 49, pp. 405-410.

Atkinson, J.W. and E.L. Walker. "The Affiliation Motive and Perceptual Sensitivity to Faces." *Journal of Abnormal and Social Psychology*, 1956, 53, pp. 38-41.

Atkinson, J.W. and W.R. Reitman. "Performance as a Function of Motive Strength and Expectancy of Goal Attainment." *Journal of Abnormal and Social Psychology*, 1956, 53, pp. 361-366.

Atkinson, J.W. *Motives in Fantasy, Action, and Society*. Princeton: Van Nostrand, 1958.

Atkinson, J.W. *An Introduction to Motivation*. Princeton: Van Nostrand, 1964.

Atkinson, J.W. and N.T. Feather. *A Theory of Achievement Motivation*. New York: John Wiley & Sons, 1966.

Atkinson, J.W. "Motivational Determinants of Risk Taking Behavior." In J.W. Atkinson and N.T. Feather (Eds) *A Theory of Achievement Motivation*. New York: John Wiley & Sons, 1966, pp. 11-30.

Atkinson, J.W. and J.O. Raynor. (Eds). *Motivation and Achievement*. Washington, D.C.: V.H. Winston (Distributed by Halsted Press of John Wiley & Co.), 1974.

Baruch, Rhoda. "The Achievement Motive in College Women." Unpublished paper, Harvard University, 1963. In D.C. McClelland and R.S. Steele (Eds) *Human Motivation: A Book of Readings*. Morristown, New Jersey: General Learning Press, 1973, pp. 203-231.

Bass, B.M. and G.V. Barrett. *Organizations*. Boston: Allyn and Bacon, Inc., 1972.

Bennis, W.G. "Conversation with Warren Bennis." *Organization Dynamics*. 1974, 2, pp. 51-66.

Berelson, B. and G.A. Steiner. *Human Behavior*. New York: Harcourt Brace and World, Inc., 1964.

Bloom, A.R. "Achievement Motivation and Occupational Choice: A Study of Adolescent Girls." Unpublished Doctoral Dissertation, Bryan Marr College, 1971.

Boyatzis, R.D. "The Need for Close Relationships and the Manager's Job." In D.A. Kolb, Irwin M. Rubin, and J. M. McIntyre (Eds) *Organizational Psychology: A Book of Readings*.

Englewood Cliffs, New Jersey: Prentice-Hall, 1974, pp. 183-188.

Bowen, D.D. "Reported Patterns in TAT Measures of Needs for Achievement, Affiliation, and Power." *Journal of Personality Assessment.* 1973, 37, pp. 424-430.

Brenner, Marshall H. "Management Development for Women." *Personnel Journal,* March, 1972, pp. 165-169.

Burdick, H.A. and A.J. Burnes. "A Test of Strain Toward Symmetry Theories." *Journal of Abnormal and Social Psychology,* 1958, 57, pp. 368-370.

Business Week. "Up the Ladder, Finally," Nov., 1975, pp. 58-68.

Chapman, J.B. "Comparison of Male and Female Leadership Styles." *Academy of Management Journal,* 1975, 18, pp. 645-650.

Christie, R. and F.L. Geis. "Studies in Machiavellianism." In J. Marecek "Power and Women's Psychological Disorder." Paper presented at the American Psychological Association, Chicago, 1975.

Clark, R.A. and D.C. McClelland. "A Factor Analytical Integration of Imaginative and Performance Measures of the Need for Achievement." *Journal of General Psychology,* 1956, 55, pp. 73-83.

Crandall, V.J., W. Katkowsky, and A. Preston. "Motivational and Ability Determinants of Young Children's Intellectual Achievement Behaviors." *Child Development,* 1962, 33, pp. 643-661.

Crockett, H.J. "The Achievement Motive and Differential Occupational Mobility in the United States." *American Sociological Review,* 1962, 27, pp. 191-204.

Crowne, D.P. and D. Marlowe. *The Approval Motive.* New York: John Wiley, 1964.

Cummin, P.C. "TAT Correlates of Executive Performance." *Journal of Applied Psychology,* 1967, 51, pp. 78-81.

DeCharms, R. "Affiliation Motivation and Productivity in Small Groups." *Journal of Abnormal and Social Psychology,* 1957, 55, pp. 222-226.

DeCharms, R. and G.H. Moeller. "Values Expressed in American Children's Readers." *Journal of Abnormal and Social Psychology,* 1962, 64, pp. 136-142.

Ellman, Edgar S. *Managing Women in Business.* (Waterford, Conn: National Foremen's Institute Bureau of Business Practice, National Sales Development Institute), 1963.

Etzioni, A. *A Comparative Analysis of Complex Organizations.* New York: The Free Press, 1961.

Exline, R.V. "Effects of Sex, Norms, and Affiliation Motivation upon Accuracy of Perception of Interpersonal Preference." *Journal of Personality,* 1960, 28, pp. 397-412.

Exline, R.V. "Need Affiliation as Initial Communication Behavior in Problemsolving Groups Characterized by Low Interpersonal Visibility." *Psychological Report,* 1962, 10, pp. 79-89.

Feld, Sheila and Charles Smith. "An Evaluation of the Objectivity of Content Analysis." In J.W. Atkinson (Ed) *Motives in Fantasy, Action, and Society.* Princeton: Van Nostrand, 1958, pp. 234-241.

French, E.G. "Motivation as a Variable in Work Partner Selection." *Journal of Abnormal and Social Psychology*, 1956, 53, pp. 96-99.

French, E.G. and F.H. Thomas. "The Relation of Achievement Motivation to Problem Solving Effectiveness." *Journal of Abnormal and Social Psychology*, 1958, 56, pp. 46-48.

French, E.G. "The Interaction of Achievement Motivation and Ability in Problem Solving Success." *Journal of Abnormal and Social Psychology*, 1958, 57, pp. 306-309.

French, J.R.P. and B. Raven. "The Bases of Social Power." In D. Cartwright and A.F. Zander (Eds) *Group Dynamics*. Evanston, Illinois: Row, Peterson, and Company, 1960, pp. 607-623.

Frerking, R.A. "Occupational Status of the Mother as a Determinant of Achievement Motivation in Women." Unpublished Doctoral Dissertation, University of Alabama, 1974.

Garfinkle, Stuart H. "Occupations of Women and Black Workers, 1962-74." *Monthly Labor Review*, November, 1975, pp. 25-35.

Grossman, Allyson Sherman. "Women in the Labor Force: The Early Years." *Monthly Labor Review*, November, 1975, pp. 3-9.

Harlow, H.F. "The Nature of Love." *American Psychologist*, 1958, 13, pp. 673-685.

Harris, Louis. *The Virginia Slims American Women's Opinion Poll.* New York, 197..

Herzberg, Frederick, B. Mausner, and Synderman. *The Motivation to Work.* New York: John Wiley and Sons, 1959.

Heyns, Roger W., Joseph Veroff, and J.W. Atkinson. "A Scoring Manual for the Affiliation Motive." In J.W. Atkinson (Ed) *Motives in Fantasy, Action, and Society*. Princeton, New Jersey: Van Nostrand, 1958, pp. 179-294.

Higginson, M.V. and T.L. Quick. *The Ambitious Women's Guide to a Successful Career.* AMACOM, 1975.

Hollander, E.P. and R.A. Willis. "Some Current Issues in the Psychology of Conformity and Non-conformity." *Psychological Bulletin*, 1967, 68, pp. 62-76.

Horowitz, R. "nAch Correlates and the Executive Role." In G.H. Litwin and Robert A. Stringer. *Motivation and Organizational Climate*. Boston: Division of Research, Harvard Business School, 1968.

Jacobs, S.L. "Achievement Motivation and Relevant Achievement Contexts: A Revived Methodology." Unpublished Doctoral Dissertation, University of Nebraska, 1971.

Jahode, M. "Conformity and Independence." *Human Relations*, 1959, 12, pp. 98-100.

Kagan, J. and H.A. Moss. "Stability and Validity of Achievement Fantasy." *Journal of Abnormal and Social Psychology*, 1959, 58, pp. 357-363.

Kagan, J. and H.A. Moss. *Birth to Maturity.* New York: John Wiley and Sons, 1962.

Klein, Deborah. "Women in the Labor Force: The Middle Years." *Monthly Labor Review*, November, 1975, pp. 10-16.

Knotts, Rose. "Manifest Needs of Professional Female Workers in Business Oriented Occupations." *Journal of Business Research,* 1975, 3, pp. 267-276.

Kolb, D.A. and R.E. Boyatzis. "On the Dynamics of the Helping Relationship." In D.A. Kolb, I.M. Rubin, and J.M. McIntyre (Eds) *Organizational Psychology: A Book of Readings.* Englewood Cliffs, New Jersey: Prentice-Hall, 1974, pp. 371-387.

Korman, Abraham K. *Industrial and Organizational Psychology.* Englewood Cliffs, New Jersey: Prentice-Hall, 1971.

Lawrence, P.R. and J.W. Lorsch. "New Management Job: The Integrator." *Harvard Business Review,* 1967, 45, pp. 142-151.

Lesser, G.S. "Achievement Motivation in Women." In D.C. McClelland and R.S. Steele (Eds) *Human Motivation: A Book of Readings.* Morristown, New Jersey: General Learning Press, 1973, pp. 203-231.

Litwin, G.H. and R.A. Stringer. *Motivation and Organizational Climate.* Boston: Harvard University, Graduate School of Business Administration, Division of Research, 1968.

Litwin, G.H. "A Note on Achievement Motivation of Salesmen and Sales Manager." In H. Heckhausen, *The Anatomy of Achievement Motivation.* New York: Academic Press, 1967.

Lowell, E.L. "The Effect of Need for Achievement on Learning and Speed of Performance." *Journal of Psychology,* 1952, 33, pp. 31-40.

Maccoby, E.E. "Developmental Psychology." *Annual Review of Psychology,* 1964, 15, pp. 203-250.

McClelland, D.C., J.W. Atkinson, R.A. Clark, and E.L. Lowell. *The Achievement Motive.* New York: Appleton-Century-Crofts, 1953.

McClelland, D.C. and J.W. Atkinson. "The Effect of Different Intensities of the Hunger Drive on Thematic Apperception." In J.W. Atkinson (Ed) *Motives in Fantasy, Action, and Society.* Princeton: Van Nostrand, 1958, pp. 46-63.

McClelland, D.C. *The Achieving Society.* Princeton, New Jersey: Van Nostrand, 1961.

McClelland, D.C. "Business Drive and National Achievement." *Harvard Business Review,* July-August, 1962, pp. 99-112.

McClelland, D.C. "Need Achievement and Entrepreneurship: A Longitudinal Study." *Journal of Personality and Social Psychology,* 1965, 1, pp. 389-392.

McClelland, D.C. "Achievement Motivation Can Be Developed." *Harvard Business Review,* 1965, 43, pp. 6-24.

McClelland, D.C. and D.G. Winter. *Motivating Economic Achievement.* New York: The Free Press, 1969.

McClelland, D.C. "The Two Faces of Power." *Journal of International Affairs,* 1970, 24, pp. 29-47.

McClelland, D.C. *Assessing Human Motivation*. New York: General Learning Press, 1971.

McClelland, D.C. and D.H. Burnham. "Power Is the Great Motivator." *Harvard Business Review*, March, 1976, pp. 100-110.

McEaddy, Beverly J. "Women in the Labor Force: The Later Years." *Monthly Labor Review*, November, 1975, pp. 17-24.

Mead, Margaret. *Male and Female*. New York: Morrow, 1949.

Mead, M. "Marriage and Family: From Popping the Question to Popping the Pill." *McCalls*, April, 1976, p. 166.

Mehrabian, A. "Male and Females Tendency to Achieve." *Educational and Psychological Measurement*, 1968, 28, pp. 493-502.

Meyer, H.H., W.B. Walker, and G.G. Litwin. "Motive Patterns and Risk Preferences Associated with Entrepreneurship." *Journal of Abnormal and Social Psychology*, 1961, 63, pp. 570-574.

Meyer, Pearl. "Women Executives Are Different."*Duns Review*, January, 1975, p. 46-48.

Misumi, J. and F. Seki. "Effects of Achievement Motivation on the Effectiveness of Leadership Patterns." *Administrative Science Quarterly*, 1971, 16, pp. 51-59.

Murray, E.J. *Motivation and Emotion*. Englewood Cliffs, New Jersey: Prentice-Hall, 1964.

Murray, H.A. *Explorations in Personality*. New York: Oxford University Press, 1938.

Noujaim, K. "Some Motivation Determinants of Effort Allocation and Performance." (Ph.D. thesis, Sloan School of Management, MIT, 1968). Cited in David A. Kolb et al., *Organizational Psychology: An Experimental Approach*, Englewood Cliffs, New Jersey: Prentice-Hall, 1971.

Podhoretz, Harriette. "Motivation of Female Doctoral Students: Manifest Needs, Perceived Parenting, and Locus of Control." Unpublished Doctoral Dissertation, Fordham University, 1974.

Parrish, John B. "Women in Professional Training." *Monthly Labor Review*, May, 1974, pp. 41-43.

Prewitt, Lena B. "The Employment Rights of the Female." Speech delivered at the Personnel Meeting of the Southeastern Electric Exchange, Baton Rouge, La: October, 1973.

Robie, Edward A. "Challenge to Management." In Eli Ginzberg and Alice M. Yohalem (Eds) *Corporate Lib: Women's Challenge to Management*. Baltimore: The Johns Hopkins University Press, 1973.

Reif, William E., John W. Newstrom, and Robert M. Monezka. "Exploding Some Myths About Women Managers." *California Management Review*, 1975, 17, pp. 72-79.

Rosen, B.C. and R.C. D'Andrade. "The Psychological Origins of Achievement Motivation." *Sociometry*, 1959, 22, pp. 185-218.

Rosen, B. and T.H. Jerdee. "The Influence of Sex-Role Stereotypes on Evaluation of Male and Female Supervisory Behavior." *Journal of Applied Psychology*, 1973, 57, pp. 44-48.

Rosenfield, H. "Social Choice Conceived as a Level of Aspiration." *Journal of Abnormal and Social Psychology,* 1964, 3, pp. 491-499.

Rosenkrantz, P., S. Vogel, H. Bee, I. Broverman, and D. Broverman, "Sex-Role Stereotypes and Self-Concepts in College Students." *Journal of Consulting and Clinical Psychology,* 1968, 32, pp. 287-295.

Sanford, F.H. and L.S. Wrightsman. *Psychology.* California: Brooks/Cole, 1970.

Schachter, S. *The Psychology of Affiliation.* Stanford University Press, 1959.

Schein, V.E. "The Relationship Between Sex-Role Stereotypes and Requisite Management Characteristics." *Journal of Applied Psychology,* 1973, 57, pp. 95-100.

Schein, V.E. "Relationship Between Sex-Role Stereotypes and Requisite Management Characteristics Among Female Managers." *Journal of Applied Psychology,* 1975, 60, pp. 340-344.

Schneider, Benjamin. *Staffing Organizations.* Pacific Palisades, California: Goodyear Publishing Co., Inc., 1976.

Schrage, H. "The R & D Entrepreneur Profile of Success." *Harvard Business Review,* November-December, 1965, pp. 56-69.

Shaw, M.C. and B.E. Dutton. "The Use of the Parent Attitude Research Inventory with Parents of Bright Academic Underachievers." *Journal of Educational Psychology,* 1962, 53, pp. 203-208.

Stein, A.H. and M.M. Bailey. "The Socialization of Achievement Orientation in Females." *Psychological Bulletin,* 1973, 80, pp. 345-366.

Stewart, A.J. "Longitudinal Predication from Personality to Life Outcomes Among College Educated Women." In D.G. Winter, *Power Motives and Power Behavior in Women.* Paper Presented at the American Psychological Association Convention, Chicago, 1975.

Stewart, A.J. "Power Arousal and Thematic Apperception." Paper presented at the American Psychological Association Convention, Chicago, 1975.

Strodtbeck, F. L. "Family Interaction, Values, and Achievement." In D.C. McClelland, et al., *Talent and Society.* Princeton: Van Nostrand, 1958, pp. 135-194.

Teahan, J.E. "Parental Attitudes and College Success." *Journal of Educational Psychology,* 1963, 54, pp. 104-109.

Vernon, M.D. *Human Motivation.* London: Cambridge University Press, 1969.

Veroff, Joseph. "Development and Validation of Projective Measure of Power Motivation." *Journal of Abnormal and Social Psychology,* 1957, 54, pp. 1-9.

Veroff, Joseph. "Development and Validation of a Projective Measure of Power Motivation." In J.W. Atkinson (Ed) *Motives in Fantasy, Action, and Society.* Princeton: Van Nostrand, 1958, pp. 105-116.

Veroff, Joseph and T.E. Shipley, Jr. "A Projective Measure of Need for Affiliation." In J.W. Atkinson (Ed) *Motives in Fantasy, Action, and Society.* Princeton: Van Nostrand, 1958, pp. 83-94.

GRAPHY** 145

Veroff, Joseph, J.W. Atkinson, Sheila C. Feld, and G. Gurin. "The Use of Thematic Apperception to Assess Motivation in a Nationwide Interview Study." *Psychological Monographs*, 1960, 94 (12, Whole No. 499).

Wainer, H.A. and I.M. Rubin. "Motivation of Research and Development Entrepreneurs: Determinants of Company Success." *Journal of Applied Psychology*, 1969, 53, pp. 178-184.

Waldman, Elizabeth and Beverly J. McEaddy. "Where Women Work." *Monthly Labor Review*, May, 1974, pp. 3-13.

Walker, E.L. and R.W. Heyns. *An Anatomy for Conformity*. Englewood Cliffs, New Jersey: Prentice-Hall, 1962.

Weber, M. *The Theory of Social and Economic Organization*. Translated by T. Parsons and A.H. Henderson, London: Oxford University Press, 1947.

Weiner, B. and A. Kulka. "An Attributional Analysis of Achievement Motivation." *Journal of Personality and Social Psychology*, 1970, 15, pp. 1-20.

Whyte, W.H. *The Organization Man*. New York: Simon and Schuster, 1956.

Wilsnack, S. "The Effects of Social Drinking on Women's Fantasy." *Journal of Personality*, 1974, 42, pp. 43-61.

Winter, D.G. "Power Motives and Power Behavior in Women." Paper presented at the American Psychological Association Convention, Chicago, 1975.

Winter, David G. *The Power Motive*. New York: The Free Press, Collier-MacMillan Publishers, 1973.

Winterbottom, M.R. "The Relation of Need for Achievement to Learning Experience in Independence and Mastery." In J.W. Atkinson (Ed) *Motives in Fantasy, Action, and Society*. Princeton: Van Nostrand, 1958, pp. 453-478.

Women's Work has Just Begun. Report on the Conference on the Redesigning of Work. The New School, New York, September 17, 1973.

AUTHOR INDEX

Adler, A., 23, 33, 139
Anderson, B.A., 18, 31, 32, 139
Andrews, J., 6, 11, 21, 30, 34, 139
Atkinson, J.W., 11, 13, 28, 30, 32, 37-40, 42, 139, 140, 141, 142, 144, 145

Bailey, M.M., 18, 31, 88, 96, 144
Barrett, G.V., 15, 29, 139
Baruch, R., 18, 31, 139
Bass, B.M., 15, 29, 139
Bee, H., 144
Bennis, W. G., 22, 23, 139
Berelson, B., 31, 139
Bloom, A.R., 31, 139
Boyatzis, R.D., 32, 139, 142
Bowen, D.D., 92, 93, 96, 140
Brenner, M.H., 10, 140
Broverman, D., 144
Broverman, I., 144
Burdick, H.A., 32, 140
Burnes, A.J., 32, 140
Burnham, D.H., 34, 143

Chapman, J.B., 10, 140
Christie, R., 33, 140
Clark, R.A., 29, 140, 142
Crandall, V.J., 17, 30, 140
Crockett, H.J., 29, 140
Crowne, D.P., 20, 31, 140
Cummin, P.C., 6, 11, 21, 30, 32, 34, 35, 42, 140

D'Andrade, R.C., 14, 28, 143
DeCharms, R., 14, 28, 32, 140
Dutton, B.E., 30, 144

Ellman, E.S., 10, 140
Etzioni, A., 33, 140
Exline, R.V., 7, 11, 32, 140

Feather, N.T., 13, 28, 139
Feld, S., 37, 42, 140, 145
French, E.G., 11, 15, 16, 29, 32, 96, 141
French, J.R.P., 23, 33, 141
Frerking, R.A., 31, 141

Garfinkle, S.H., 1, 9, 141
Geis, F.L., 33, 140
Grossman, A.S., 9, 141
Gurin, G., 37, 145

Harlow, H.F., 19, 31, 141
Harris, L., 91, 96, 141
Herzberg, F., 91, 96, 141
Heyns, R.W., 10, 31, 42, 139, 141, 145
Higginson, M.V., 10, 141
Hollander, E.P., 32, 141
Horowitz, R., 30, 141

Jacobs, S.L., 18, 31, 141
Jahode, M., 32, 141
Jerdee, T.H., 4, 10, 143

Kagan, J., 17, 28, 30, 141
Katkowsky, W., 140
Klein, D., 2, 9, 141
Knotts, R., 10, 18, 31, 142
Kolb, D.A., 32, 139, 142, 143
Korman, A.K., 42, 142
Kulka, A., 29, 145

Lawrence, P.R., 22, 32, 142
Lesser, G.S., 17, 31, 142
Litwin, G.H., 14, 16, 21, 24, 28-30, 32, 33, 142, 143
Lorsch, J.W., 22, 32, 142
Lowell, E.L., 29, 142

Maccoby, E.E., 30, 142
McClelland, D.C., 5, 6, 10, 11, 13-17, 21, 25, 28-30, 32-35, 36, 39, 40, 42, 94, 96, 139, 140, 142, 143
McDowell, W.J., 18, 31, 139
McEaddy, B.J., 1, 2, 9, 143, 145
McIntyre, J.M., 32, 139, 142
Marlowe, D., 20, 140
Mead, M., 30, 34, 143
Mehrabian, A., 15, 29, 143
Meyer, H.H., 14, 21, 28, 29, 32, 143
Meyer, P., 9, 143
Missumi, J., 16, 30, 143
Moeller, G.H., 14, 28, 140
Monezka, R.M., 4, 143
Moss, H.A., 17, 28, 30, 141
Murray, E.J., 32, 143
Murray, H.A., 5, 10, 143

Newstrom, J.W., 4, 143
Noujaim, K., 29, 143

Podhoretz, H., 18, 31, 143
Parrish, J.B., 9, 143

SUBJECT INDEX

Achievement motivation, 5-7, 13-21, 24,
    25, 27, 35, 36, 39-41, 45-55, 87-95
  and age, 13, 52-53, 55, 92
  and alcohol, 54
  and careers, 15, 87
  definition of, 5, 13, 39
  and education, 15, 17, 18, 27, 52,
    55, 91
  and entrepreneurs, 15, 17
  and females, 17-19, 27
  and income, 53
  and leadership styles, 16
  and managers and executives, 15, 16,
    21, 90
  and parental influence, 14, 17, 18
  and performance, 15, 17, 21, 88
  and rewards, 16
  and risk, 14, 15
  and scoring criteria, 39-41
  and smoking, 54, 55, 92
  and society, 14
  and success, 15, 25
  and task, 16
  and women managers, 7, 35, 45-55,
    87-95
Affiliation motivation, 5-7, 16, 18-22, 27,
    35, 36, 39-41, 45-55, 87-95
  and age, 52, 92
  and alcohol, 54, 55
  and conformity, 20
  definition of, 5, 19, 39
  and education, 52, 91
  and females, 18, 22, 27
  and income, 53, 55, 92
  and managers and executives, 21
  and parental influence, 19
  and performance, 21, 22
  and scoring criteria, 39-41
  and smoking, 54
  and task, 16
  and women managers, 6, 35, 45-55,
    87-95

Edwards Personal Preference Schedule
    (EPPS), 18
Entrepreneurs, 15, 17, 25
Equal Employment legislation, 1

Machiavellian power, 23
Maleocracy, 1
Motivation (*See* Achievement, Affiliation
    and Power Motivation)

  and strength, 6
  and scoring criteria, 6

Power Motivation, 5-7, 17, 22-27, 35, 36,
    39-41, 45-55, 87-95
  and age, 26, 52, 92
  and alcohol, 26, 54
  and bases of power, 23
  and career, 24-26
  definition of, 6, 22, 23, 39
  and education, 26, 52, 91
  and entrepreneurs, 25
  and females, 26, 27
  and income, 53
  and managers and executives, 17, 24, 25
  and performance, 24, 25
  and scoring criteria, 39-41
  and smoking, 54-55
  and women managers, 6, 35, 45-55,
    87-95

Thematic Apperception Test (TAT), 6, 26,
    36-41, 95

Women:
  and career, 3, 26
  and education, 2, 19, 22, 26, 27
  and income level, 3
  and the labor force, 1-3
  and management, 4, 19, 27
  and occupation, 2-4
Women managers:
  and achievement motivation, 7, 35, 45-
    55, 87-95
  and affiliation motivation, 7, 35, 45-55,
    87-95
  and age, 35, 36, 52, 55, 92
  and career, 87
  and educational level, 35-37, 52, 55, 91,
    92
  and income level, 37, 53, 55, 92
  and performance, 88
  and power motivation, 7, 35, 45-55,
    87-95
  and preference for co-workers, 7, 35,
    46-48, 50, 51, 55, 87, 89, 91, 95
  and preference for subordinates, 7, 35,
    46-48, 50, 51, 55, 87, 89, 91, 95
  and preference for superiors, 7, 35,
    46-48, 50, 51, 55, 87, 89, 91, 95
  and manufacturing sector, 35, 45-55,
    87-92
  and service sector, 35, 45-55, 87-92, 95
  and smoking, 54, 92